UNVEILED

How Western Liberals
Empower Radical Islam

YASMINE MOHAMMED

UNVEILED

How Western Liberals
Empower Radical Islam

YASMINE MOHAMMED

Free Hearts Free Minds

126-1644 Hillside Ave

PO Box 35054 RPO Hillside

Victoria BC

V8T 5G2

www.freeheartsfreeminds.com

Library and Archives Canada Cataloguing in Publication
Title: Unveiled: how western liberals empower radical Islam / Yasmine Mohammed.
Names: Mohammed, Yasmine, 1974- author. | Free Hearts Free Minds (Organization), publisher.
Identifiers: Canadiana (print) 20190174986 | Canadiana (ebook) 20190174994 | ISBN 9781999240509
(Softcover) | ISBN 9781999240516 (PDF)
Subjects: LCSH: Mohammed, Yasmine, 1974- | LCSH: Muslim women—Canada—Biography. | LCSH: Muslims—
Western countries—Social conditions. | LCSH: Islam—Western countries—Public opinion. | LCSH: Islamic fundamentalism. | LCSH: Islam—Customs and practices. | LCGFT: Autobiographies.
Classification: LCC FC106.M9 Z7 2019 | DDC 305.48/697092—dc23
Printed in Canada

All those interested in how humans overcome adversity must read this book. Yasmine is one of the bravest people of our time. She is a shining example to all of us.

Ayaan Hirsi Ali, author of *Infidel*

Too many of us fail to realize that the principal victims of the unspeakable cruelty that fervent adherence to Islam inspires (not to mention the bossy control-freakery that invades even minute details of everyday life) are Muslims themselves. Especially women. Yasmine Mohammed's heartrending, brave, and beautifully written book brings this home in a way that should finally change the minds of even the most deeply misguided apologists in our well-meaning liberal midst.

Richard Dawkins, author of *The God Delusion*

Women and freethinkers in traditional Muslim communities inherit a double burden. If they want to live in the modern world, they must confront not only the theocrats in their homes and schools, but many secular liberals—whose apathy, sanctimony, and hallucinations of "racism" throw yet another veil over their suffering. In Unveiled, Yasmine Mohammed accepts this challenge as courageously as anyone I've ever met, putting the lie to the dangerous notion that criticizing the doctrine of Islam is a form of bigotry. Let her wisdom and bravery inspire you.

Sam Harris, author of *The End of Faith*

Insider personal accounts form powerful testimonies. Deeply moving, at times depressing but filled with hope for what can be, instead of what is, Yasmine's story is no exception. Ex-Muslim women are likely to be the most oppressed minority group around the world. Name one other personal choice that can lead to honour-based violence coupled with mob execution in countries that we consider our allies. No liberal is worth their salt if they neglect these minorities within minorities. And Muslims worldwide must recognize this tyranny within our ranks. I hope Yasmine's brave personal account can contribute to raising such desperately needed awareness.

Maajid Nawaz, author of *Radical*

Yasmine Mohammed is a very courageous woman and a shining example for all women who have faced abuse either under the guise of religion or culture. Yasmine's story is tragic and compelling at the same time. She weathered something no human should endure. Her story is also one of tenacity and courage because "There is no excuse for Abuse"

Raheel Raza, author of *Their Jihad, not my Jihad*

TABLE OF CONTENTS

For Tiffers

DEDICATION

This book is for every person who feels crushed under the enormous pressure and terrifying threats of Islam. I hope my story helps you and inspires you to break free and spread your own gorgeous wings.

This book is also for those of you who feel compelled to demonize all Muslims. I hope you will see that we are all just human beings and that we all battle our own demons.

This book is for anyone who feels a duty to defend Islam from scrutiny and criticism. I hope you will see that whenever you deflect criticism, you are deflecting the light from shining on millions of people imprisoned in darkness.

And last, but most definitely not least, this book is for my fellow warriors. My fellow ex-Muslims, my fellow atheists, my fellow freethinkers, and my fellow troublemakers.

FOREWORD

By Rick Fabbro

At 11:26 a.m. on July 17, 2018, my phone dinged. I am never sure which ding is associated with which app so I started scrolling through email, Facebook, Twitter, the word games I play with my friends; finally I opened a messaging text.

"Hi Mr. Fabbro. I was your Gr 8 Drama student in 1988/89 . . . I am not sure if you remember me . . ."

Upon reading the message my heart took a little skip. Quiet tears wetted my cheeks.

"Yasmine, not only do I remember you, I have thought about you many, many times over the last 30 years!"

With intense clarity, a memory once again came to mind of a courageous thirteen-year-old girl sitting across from me in my office describing horrors perpetrated upon her that challenge one's ability to believe that a human being could be so cruel to another, let alone another so helpless and harmless. She pledged determination to take her story to the authorities who would rescue her from her dreadful homelife.

Authorities were engaged, and I didn't see her again. I assumed she was whisked off to a safe home and eventually all would be well. At the end of the year, I transferred to a different school and was left wondering about how Yasmine's future played out.

"I just wanted to say thank you. Things didn't work out, as the judge deemed it 'cultural freedom' for my family to abuse me."

My heart sank. Now, instead of merely wondering how her life evolved over the last thirty years, questions burned in me. We arranged to meet. We hugged. We talked and cried. She asked me to read a draft of this book.

Unveiled tells the whole compelling story. It answers the questions. Family forces, government forces, religious and cultural forces all tried to exert their power over her. This book, despite moments when she feels defeated, tells how her courage and determination prevail.

This is an important book not just for the gripping personal story she shares, but because her story is not unique. Yas' is a voice that must be heard by people everywhere feeling oppressed by powers hindering their opportunity to live a free life.

~ Rick Fabbro

I have found it impossible to talk to anyone about my problems. I couldn't face the embarrassment, and anyway I lack the courage. Any courage I had was knocked out of me when I was young. But now, all of sudden I have a sort of desperate wish to tell everything to somebody.

~ Roald Dahl, Matilda

PROLOGUE

The fact that I grew up Muslim should be nothing more than a distant memory. I broke away from that world in 2004. But the traumatic world I was born into has defined me. It's in my bones. It runs in my blood. I can't escape it. I had thought I could escape it. I would start over, redefine myself, live my life on my own terms. But I realized that I can't escape my own self. The very connections in my mind, the visceral reactions of my body—I have no control over any of that. And I can't reconstruct myself. At times, I think that I might have overcome it all, that I might be able to live a "normal" life. But as soon as my guard is down, a dormant memory rears its ugly head.

The soil I grew up on, the water that nourished me, it was all poisoned with deceit, fear, lies, treachery, anger, sadness, and lots and lots of abuse. I may look like a healthy tree on the outside, but the truth is hidden inside my roots. I manage to fool everyone around me. Friends who I have known for years have no clue. They say things like, "But you seem so normal!" and "How are you not a basket case?" and "I never would have guessed!"

Even my husband can't reconcile the stories of this girl whose life is so far removed from his own with the woman he fell in love with. We met a few years after I had severed ties with my family. I was by no means healed, but I had learned to swallow my pain. There was no outlet. No one would understand. I knew it made people uncomfortable to talk about Islam. So I just pushed it all aside.

It wasn't until years after I had left Islam that I would stumble upon Bill Maher's Facebook page. Ex-Muslims were responding to Ben Affleck's reaction to Sam Harris criticizing Islam. His cries of *gross and racist* are legendary now, almost cliché. I had never even heard the term ex-Muslim before that. I had no idea there were others like me. I kept my sordid secrets to myself. My life is not politically correct. I do not fit the preferred narrative. My life story is an uncomfortable truth, and people much prefer their comfortable lies. But their reaction to Ben Affleck's rant made me want to get involved.

Sam Harris, a neuroscientist and the author of a groundbreaking book called *The End of Faith*, was on Bill Maher's show in October 2014 talking about Islam in his signature commanding yet soft-spoken manner. He approached the topic with the same academic rigor he applies to any of his research on world religions. He spoke of Islam no differently than he has spoken of Christianity, Judaism, and many other religions and ideologies—by stating facts.

He and Bill Maher began the conversation by lamenting the fact that liberals are failing to stand up for liberal values. Bill recounted how his audience would raucously applaud for principles like freedom of speech, freedom of religion, and equality for women, minorities, and LGBT, but the applause would abruptly halt if anyone mentioned that these principles were not being upheld in the Muslim world. Sam added that liberals are happy to criticize white theocracies, Christian theocracies, but they fail to criticize the same evils in the Muslim world. He clarified that *Islam*, the religion (a set of ideas) was very different from *Muslims*, the people.

As if on cue, Ben Affleck, an actor who played the part of a fallen angel in the movie *Dogma*, seemingly decided to volunteer as exhibit A to embody that exact caricature of a confused liberal that Sam was referring to by hurling charges of racism at both Bill and Sam. He likened them to people who use the term *shifty Jew* or who say things like "Black people just always want to shoot each other." He insisted that Muslims "just want to eat sandwiches," illustrating exactly the hypocrisy that Sam had just outlined. Did Ben Affleck, the man who made a movie focused specifically on criticizing and mocking Christianity, feel that it was beyond the pale for Sam Harris and Bill Maher to have a civil, factual conversation about Islam?

Even though both Bill and Sam quoted statistics from the Pew Research Center—that approximately 90 percent of Egyptians believe people should be killed for leaving their religion, Ben still insisted that these bad ideas were only held by a nominal number of Muslims.

From my perspective, it was unforgivable for Ben Affleck to deflect criticism of this ideology that has caused so much suffering in the world. Generally, no one in the West cares if Muslim women were being imprisoned or killed in Iran or Saudi Arabia for not covering their hair. No one cared that bloggers in Bangladesh were being hacked to death in the streets because they dared write about humanism. No one cared if university students were beaten to death in Pakistan for questioning Islam. But now, finally, mainstream people on mainstream television were talking about these issues that have been plaguing the Muslim world for 1,400 years—and this seemingly well-meaning, white-guilt ridden man was standing in the way! I was enraged.

I remember feeling that I wanted to speak out. I wanted to shout and scream out. I wanted to join Sam Harris in this battle of ideas. However, I was also terrified. I felt like I was standing on a precipice jutting out over a vast ocean. I was safe on dry land. I had freed myself from the dangerous waters below. But I now had this overwhelming sense that I wanted to dive back in. I wanted to meet others who had been through what I had been through. I wanted to share my stories with them and with everyone. I wanted a community of people who could understand my latent fears, insecurities, and obsessions.

It was a huge risk. No one in my life knew my backstory. No one. The only person who knew had passed away years earlier. I had no life witnesses. I could continue to live in parallel to all these goings-on and choose not to step off that cliff into that ocean. I would be undetectable.

Or, I could be brave. I could choose to step in, get myself covered in saltwater and seaweed, and even risk drowning. I could choose to share my perspective. I could choose to correct friends who insisted Islam was a religion of peace. I could choose to make people uncomfortable with my story. I could choose to deal with the backlash, the friends who would walk away from me and the death threats.

A saner person would have just turned around and walked away from that ocean. I knew what was in it. I had been there before. It would have been so easy to just turn around and continue to live my life on the safe, dry land that I had already risked my life to scramble onto.

But I chose to dive in.

VIOLENCE I

"Please, no! Please, I'm sorry. Mama! Mama! Please!"

I'm lying on my bed as I was ordered, pleading frantically as I've done many times before. I'm dreading the familiar scene, even though it's unfolding right in front of me. He grabs my ankle and tugs me sharply toward the foot of the bed. I have to resist the urge to pull my feet away. I know that it will be worse if I do. I'm crying so hard I can't catch my breath as he uses my skipping rope to bind my feet to the bed.

He picks up his favourite orange plastic stick. It replaced the wood ones that kept breaking. At first I was glad, as this wouldn't give me splinters, but I didn't realize it would hurt so much more. For the rest of my life, I will hate the colour orange. He whips the soles of my feet. The soles of the feet are a preferred spot, as the scars will remain hidden from teachers. I am six years old, and this is my punishment for not correctly memorizing surahs (chapters) from the Quran.

"So, you think you'll memorize properly next time?"

"Yes!"

I plead to my mother with my eyes. *Why aren't you raising your voice or your hand to protect me? Why are you just standing there next to him?*

What could possibly be holding her back? Was she afraid of him? She had asked him to come over. Was she partly to blame? In the moment, I cannot accept that the only parent I know would willingly give me up to be bound and beaten. He is the evil one, not my mother. That had to be the truth. So why, then, had she phoned him and asked him to come over? Why?

"Next time I come here, I want to hear all three surahs, you understand?"

"Yes . . ."

"Which three surahs are they?"

I hesitate for a fraction of a second, and he raises his hand again, a hint of anticipation glinting from his eyes.

When there is no fresh skin for his blows to land on, they fall on my already bruised and torn feet. My body is slick with sweat. My heart is racing. It's difficult to breathe, but I know this will never end until I find the strength to push on.

"*Al Fatiha, Al Kauthar,* and . . . *Al Ikhlas.*" Three short surahs necessary for the five daily prayers. The words come out of me, rasping, choking, barely audible.

"If you make one mistake—one mistake—I will show you how I can really hurt you."

Finally, he unties the rope, throws it on the floor, and walks out. I lie there waiting for my mother to come and console me. She doesn't come. I wait after every beating, but she never comes. She always follows him out the door, and I listen to their voices and laughter as they tell stories. I wait breathlessly to hear the front door close. I cannot relax until I know he is out of the apartment. It's hard to steady my breathing as I watch the lights from the cars on the street below sweep across my ceiling. Swoosh, swoosh, swoosh. Eventually, I curl up into a ball and slip my thumb into my mouth.

Despite the throbbing in my feet and the involuntary sobs that inflate my chest forcefully, I fall into a deep sleep, the kind of deep sleep that can only follow a struggle that threatens to destroy your very soul.

I awaken groggily in the middle of the night with the familiar cold wet spot underneath me. One of my feet touches the spot, and the unbearable stinging forces me wide awake. I know I have to make my way to the washroom, but the thought of the pain of bearing my own weight on my torn feet makes my eyes well up with tears again. Carefully, I dangle my feet over the side of the bed. They are swollen and covered with bubbles of blood. I brace myself before stepping down. I know that if I put all my weight on them, they might burst, but I have to move quickly to wash off the pee that stings the open sores. I walk on the outer sides of my feet so that my sores can avoid the carpet. I hobble slowly, steadying myself with every step—first with my bed, then my dresser, then the doorknob, then the wall in the hallway. The sensation of the squish as the wounds inevitably tear open is one I still remember vividly almost forty years later.

All this pain is nothing, I am assured, compared to the fire of Hell if I do not memorize. Before I learn to bite my tongue, I question.

"If Allah burned my flesh off, and then regrew it, and then burned it again for all eternity, won't I eventually get used to it?"

"No," my mom replies. "Allah will make sure that every single time it hurts as much as the first time."

I was terrified of Allah, of the Day of Judgment, of burning in Hell—not things that occupy the mind of the average child, well, not the average non-Muslim child.

The Internet is full of YouTube videos of children being viciously attacked in madrasas. Girls getting grabbed by the hair and being pulled to the ground for not wearing hijab (head covers), boys being whipped and kicked as they fall to the ground. The abuse I endured, as barbaric as it was, is light in comparison to stories I've heard. A girl in Somalia told me of how her mother poured hot oil down her brother's throat (as he was tied to a bed), and the siblings were forced to watch.

According to recent reports, in the Muslim-majority countries in the Middle East and North Africa, more than 70 percent of children aged two to fourteen years are disciplined in a violent manner. In some countries—

like Yemen, Tunisia, Palestine, Egypt—over 90 percent of children report being violently abused. What is the reason for this? Why do those countries have such incidences of violence against children? The common thread is that they all follow the same religion. A religion that instructs them to beat their children. According to Hadith, the record of sayings and actions by Muhammad, he said, "Teach your children to pray when they are seven years old, and smack them if they do not do so when they are ten." (classed as saheeh by Shaykh al-Albaani in *Saheeh al-Jaami*, 5868) He also said, "Hang your whip where members of your household (your children, wife, and slaves) can see it, for that will discipline them." (said by al-Albaani in *Saheeh al-Jaami*, 4022)

You see, it is the parent's responsibility to ensure their children memorize the Quran, do not miss a daily prayer, and follow the narrow path set out for them. "Each of you is a shepherd and each of you is responsible for his flock. The ruler is a shepherd and is responsible for his flock. A man is the shepherd of his family and is responsible for his flock. A woman is the shepherd of her husband's household and is responsible for her flock. A servant is the shepherd of his master's wealth and is responsible for his flock. Each of you is a shepherd and is responsible for his flock." (narrated by al-Bukhaari, 583; Muslim, 1829)

So when parents beat their children, they do it out of religious duty and fear; they have to ensure that their children are devout Muslims. If they are not, the parents are the ones who have failed, and they will have to answer to Allah on the Day of Judgment. If their children are not devout Muslims, the parents' souls are in jeopardy of burning in Hell for eternity.

Research shows that 7 in 10 children on average are subjected to psychological aggression with the highest rate in Yemen (90 percent). Around 6 in 10 children experience physical punishment. The highest rates are in the Central African Republic, Egypt and Yemen (more than 80 percent).

For the most part, households employ a combination of violent disciplinary practices. Most children in a majority of countries or areas are exposed to both psychological as well as physical means of punishment. This confirms that these two forms of violence often overlap and frequently occur together within the context of discipline. Such exposure to multiple types of violence may exacerbate the potential harm to a child in both the short and long term.

Although the abuse and threats of abuse petrified me, I don't remember a time in my life when I didn't push back. Listening to music, for example, was forbidden. Music is from the devil. Nonetheless, when no one was home, I would turn the dial on our clock radio to LG73 and listen to the pop hits of the day. The Fresh Prince was right: parents just don't understand. But I feared the wrath of Allah. Singing along to John Lennon's "Imagine," I always fell silent when it came to the line "imagine no religion"—too scared even to hum it, lest I apostate myself. Being an apostate, a *kafir* (nonbeliever), is the worst possible sin in Islam. Punishable by death. I remember wondering, how could I love 99 percent of this song so strongly but be so completely avoidant of this one line? So avoidant I couldn't even lip-sync it. Could it be that if Lennon was right about the rest of it, maybe he was right about that line, too?

I have quite a few memories like that, of times when the light glinted momentarily through the cracks of the binding cement of Islam that was slathered on me layer after layer throughout my childhood.

PRAYER

Muslims are required to observe the Five Pillars of Islam: profession of faith, five daily prayers, alms-giving, fasting during Ramadan, and pilgrimage to Mecca. Repeating the rhythmic patterns and hypnotically moaning the foreign words during the five daily prayers keep us forever in line. No time to stray from the right path if the next prayer is constantly impending. No time for the cement to chip off before a new layer is troweled on.

The prayers are mind-numbingly repetitive. There is no room for the slightest variation. Every ceremonial motion and every word is specific and methodic, stripping the *ummah* (the community of Muslims) of any individuality. Get in line. Follow the herd. No distractions. During hajj, the holy pilgrimage to Mecca, everyone is actually stripped of their individual clothing, and all the hajjis dress alike in simple white cloth.

Preparing to pray was as repetitive a process as the prayers themselves. The first step was a washing up ritual called *wudu*. Each step of *wudu* needed to be repeated three times: wash your hands three times, rinse out your mouth three times, wipe your nose three times, wash your face three times, rinse your arms from wrist to elbow three times, wipe your ears three times, wash your feet three times.

My legs were too short to lift my feet into the sink, so I would hop up onto the counter for the last step. After *wudu*, you were ready to start praying, but if you peed or pooped or farted after *wudu*, you had to do the ritual all over again.

The prayers were next. They came with their own ritualistic minutiae. You had to be facing in a specific direction: toward the Kaaba in Mecca, Saudi Arabia. The boys didn't need to wear anything specific, but the girls had to cover every inch of their bodies except for their faces and hands. I hated wearing socks, but Allah didn't accept prayers from girls with exposed toes, only from boys.

My brother would start with the *adhan*, or call to prayer. There didn't seem to be much need for it, considering we were all there in the living room already. He would turn his head to the left and right to make sure his voice carried as far as possible.

Then we would line up—boys in front, girls behind. At the Mosque we attended, men enter from the main doors, while women enter through a rear entrance just off the kitchen, near the dumpsters. The issue with the gender segregation in Mosques has been highlighted by Muslim reformers like Asra Nomani. She wrote an article in the *Washington Post* on how she once entered a Mosque through the main doors with her father. She and her father were both harassed until she left the area and joined the women in the basement where she belonged. Women in Europe are now fighting back by not only having Mosques that are not segregated, but ones that are led by female Imams! Of course, those are not permanent Mosques. Generally, the women perform their prayers in Churches, where the gracious clergy open the doors for them on Fridays so they can worship freely without fear of retaliation. They are a small group of only women, but they are defying the gender apartheid that is widely accepted in Islam. They change the venue every week for fear of fundamentalists who send them threats for their insubordination. There are other groups of Muslims defying the fundamentalists by having Mosques that allow LGBT worshippers and even LGBT Imams! I wholeheartedly support Muslims who are open to inclusivity and who oppose discrimination.

Men generally pray together and women together. If they must be in the same room, then men are in front and women behind, usually with a divider of some sort in between them. In their separate lines, they stand as close as possible to one another, shoulders touching, feet touching, so that the devil can't get in between them.

The prayers follow a specific procedure, a series of movements. First, you stand with your hands on your chest (right hand over your left hand), and you recite a specific surah in this position. Then you put your hands on your knees and repeat another specific surah three times, then straighten up again, then go facedown on the floor, mumble the prescribed words three times, then rock back on your knees saying the words explicit for this position, then facedown on the floor again, and back up on your knees again. One of these cycles is called a rak'a. The length of the prayers differed from two to four rak'as. And after each prayer, there were extra prayers I was told were optional. They were never optional for me, though.

This entire ritual had to happen five times a day. And in each prayer, in each rak'a, the same words were repeated, chanted, burned into my brain. I never knew the meaning of any of the words that I repeated at least twenty times a day. Their meaning was never discussed. They were just meant to be repeated ad nauseam without thought. Questioning only led to anger and admonishment.

Even though the majority of the day was taken up in prayer, doubt found a way to sneak in. I wished I could just submit—that is, after all, the true meaning of the word *Islam*. Good Muslims stop struggling and just submit to the cement drying them in place.

I never did stop struggling, but I was filled with self-hatred for it. How could I ever be a true Muslim if I couldn't let go and just submit? My sister and brother didn't seem to have any problems, not that they shared with me, anyway. For this, I earned the moniker "black sheep" from my mother. She said it was the devil making me question.

As I grew older, the questions became harder to answer. I recall a particularly revealing exchange with my mother in my teen years.

"He was over fifty years old, and he married a six-year-old?"

"So? Do you think that you know more than Allah's prophet? Who are you to question his actions?"

"Was he a pedophile?"

"No! Of course not! He only had sex with her after she became a woman. After she got her period. Before that, he only did other things with her, to prepare her. So she would be comfortable with him when the day came. *Subhanallah*, Allah's messenger was always thoughtful and considerate like that."

"Oh, so she was all grown up . . . ?"

"Yes, in the eyes of Allah she was grown up. You become a woman when you get your period, and all your sins start to get counted. Before that, you are a child, and nothing you do is recorded."

"So how old was she?"

"She was nine."

"Nine? That's not a woman!" By now I was shouting.

My mother answered my persistent questions with a slap on the face, with nasty, hate-filled words and reminders that my questioning was the devil getting in my brain, whispering these thoughts to me. *Shaytan*, the devil, was too strong for me to fight. I tried to swallow my questions, but sometimes I couldn't help myself. And as the battle raged, I became too scared even to question things in my own head, as Allah would read my mind and punish me for doubting him. Anything positive was thanks to Allah, and anything negative was because of my weakness, because of the devil influencing me. I never felt in control of my own life.

It wasn't the devil, of course. It was natural questioning and critical thinking.

This was one of the most difficult things about leaving Islam—making decisions, relying on my inner thoughts and voice that had been regularly stifled in the past. Now I had to conjure them up again and figure out how to hear and trust myself. I was not taught to think. Thinking was discouraged and, in fact, punished. I was taught to do as I was told. Every single aspect of life was prescribed for me. No decision was mine to make: how to use the bathroom, how to drink water, how to cut my nails, how to put on my shoes—and everything in between—was specifically outlined. I was nothing more than a vessel created to spread the word of Allah, and, hopefully, to give my life in that endeavour—the perfect life of a good Muslim, no more, no less.

SUBMISSION I

I was never happy with the role I'd been cast in. I remembered a time when I was free of any cement, before that hideous man entered our lives, and so I struggled with each layer that was piled on me. I remembered the years before my mother met him and embraced fundamentalist Islam and started covering her hair and calling everything haram (forbidden) I remembered taking swimming lessons and playing in the park. I remembered not having to get up before dawn to mumble into the carpet. I remembered being allowed to play with my Barbies and with the non-Muslim neighbour's kids. I remembered celebrating birthdays and swimming and eating Oreos. All of these things and so much more were now forbidden.

Even though I was living in Canada, my mother had not even been raised like this in Egypt. I would stare with envy at my parents' black-and-white wedding photos. My mother looked like a Bond girl in her knee-length wedding gown. She wore her hair in a beehive, and she had dramatic eye makeup with huge, swooping fake lashes. A gorgeous and elegant belly dancer could be seen in almost every photograph. I used to look at those wedding photos and be struck with what a completely different world she had come from.

So many things in that four-by-six-inch frame were haram. My mother's legs were bare, her dress was tight, her sleeves only reached her elbow, she wore makeup, and her hair was uncovered. Even her hairstyle was forbidden in Islam. There was alcohol, music, and dancing: all of those things are haram.

My mom probably never even heard the word *haram* growing up. She had lived a charmed life. Her father's uncle was the first president of Egypt, so they were filthy rich and powerful. My grandfather was already married with three children when his uncle became the most powerful man in the country. However, he decided to capitalize on his new-found celebrity and get himself a light-skinned wife. He needed his trophy wife to have European colouring and features, but she still had to be the right religion, so he got himself a young girl from Turkey as his second (concurrent) wife.

When my grandmother arrived in Egypt, she didn't even speak Arabic, but she was richly rewarded for her efforts. She moved into a huge mansion with multiple servants and proceeded to push out children—seven, to be exact. When Nasser came into power, and my grandfather's uncle became persona non grata and was put under house arrest, it all became too much for my grandfather. He was already feeling overwhelmed with a total of ten children and two wives, so he moved to Saudi Arabia. I have heard family members speculate that he didn't need to move, but that it was just an excuse to get away from all of his familial responsibilities. From there, he sent money to his two families. Of course, he wasn't about to be all alone over there, so he married a third time.

He didn't move away until my mother was in university, though. There was no question that my mom was the favourite. As the first of seven children, she and her twin sister were the only ones who were actually raised by their father. None of the other kids were as lucky; some of them barely even remember their father. She had nannies her whole life. She never had to lift a finger. The (true) joke was that when she married my dad, she didn't even know how to boil water. She went to fancy private Catholic schools. In those days in Egypt, people were much more secular than they are now. These were the days before the rise of the Muslim Brotherhood.

Now, unfortunately, Egyptian Christians are killed by the hundreds as they pray in their churches. And even Muslims not deemed Muslim enough by the Sunni extremists, such as Sufi Muslims, are killed in Egypt as they worship in their Mosques. The whole Middle East and North Africa have become more extreme, and those extremists are spreading into Europe and North America as well. Other sects of Muslims are not even tolerated. An Ahmadi shopkeeper in the UK was killed by a Sunni extremist because he wished his patrons "Happy Easter." Sunnis are the majority of Muslims (about 90 percent) with Shias being the next largest sect (almost 10 percent) and all the remaining sects together barely 1 percent. Generally, in this book, when I refer to "Muslims," I am referring to the overwhelming majority of Sunni Muslims—as that is my experience. In my mother's day, it was common for people to identify loosely as Muslim but not take their religion so seriously. Women did not wear hijab, people would drink, and Islam was as casual as religion is for most Christians today. But things have changed significantly.

I was angry that my mother had gotten to live such a glamorous life while I was forced to study *surahs* from the *Quran*, not allowed to ride a bike for fear I might lose my virginity or learn to swim because bathing suits showed too much skin. Why didn't she want me to have the same freedoms she had? She had Christian friends, but I wasn't even allowed to play with my friends down the hall, Chelsea and Lindsay, because they were *kuffar*, non-believers. Day after day, they would knock on the apartment door.

"Can we come in and play with Yasmine?"

"No, not right now," my mother would answer. I would stand in the hallway, wringing my hands, desperately hoping she would relent.

"Can she come to our place?"

"No, she's busy."

"I'm not busy!" I'd chirp.

"Go to your room!"

I often wonder how different I would be if our lives were never ruined by an atomic bomb that went off in our home.

That bomb was the man who took my mother as his second wife—"Uncle" Mounir. His entrance into our life was truly explosive. No tremble, no warning, no change of wind—just suddenly there, a violent sociopath tearing through our life. He walked into our home like he owned it, with his disheveled beard and his calloused hands. He rarely interacted with me, unless it was to bind my feet to the foot of my bed. I had no idea my mother was a second wife. We called him *uncle*, and he had his own wife and children. It wasn't until I was in college that my mother finally revealed this truth. Polygamy is against the law in the liberal democracy of Canada, and so she didn't trust us children with that damning information. Little did she know that our government routinely turns a blind eye to Muslim men with multiple wives. Millions of dollars of government funds are being funneled to support a man who is breaking the law. If a man can't afford to support all his wives, he simply gets them to all apply for social assistance as single mothers, and voila! Problem solved. My mother was one such woman. Because she was only Islamically, not legally, married to him, she could collect social assistance as a single mother and the government ignored the fact that she was married to this man because to question it would be racist or something.

Even though he was technically a stepfather to me, I never called him that. And we never had a father-daughter relationship. He was just the man who would beat us, and (I would learn later) occasionally have sex with our mother.

Sometimes I would come home from school to find him in my home.

"What did I do?" As far as I knew, the only purpose of his visits was to beat someone.

"Nothing. Just go play in your room." My mom would shoo me off.

One time I went to use the bathroom, and I heard them both in the shower. No biggie. My brother and I used to bathe together in those days. Later, in front of his wife—I can't remember why—I happened to mention that they were in the shower together.

"What? That's not true!" He and my mom both vehemently denied it.

"Yes, you were. I heard you both in there." They inexplicably kept insisting that I was mistaken. And I couldn't figure out why.

It's a weird feeling to know that your mother is lying. I didn't think she was capable of it. They kept insisting that I was wrong. Eventually, I found myself agreeing with her, even though it contradicted what was right in front of me. I didn't see what I saw, or hear what I heard, because she told me differently. And I had to believe her. She was my mother, after all. I trusted her more than myself. So I relented and accepted that they weren't in the shower together. I must have been mistaken.

I got the same feeling when she told me that she would talk to him and ask him to stop beating us. And I believed her. Even though he would be right back there again the next day. How could he have known if we'd missed a prayer? He wasn't even there. Somehow, the words she said had this power to override reality.

Before he invaded our home, we lived a much calmer life. We had an outdoor pool in our building. I had just learned to swim underwater—I wasn't yet confident with a front crawl, but I was determined to learn. We also had a playground in our building that I would play in for hours. I would ride my bike and play Barbies with my friends. My siblings and I had a lot of freedom. We were too young to recognize that the freedom was actually neglect; we just thought it meant we could stay out and play for as long as we wanted. When all my friends had gone in for dinner and there was no one left to play with, I would go back upstairs. But there was never any dinner waiting on our dining table.

"Don't you have to go home now?" my friend's mother would say.

"No, I can stay for as long as I want."

"When is your bedtime?"

"I don't have one!" I'd reply proudly.

"You're so lucky," my friend would respond.

My mom spent most of her days watching soap operas and eating sunflower seeds. I would leave for school in the morning and return to find her in the same spot, the only difference being that the mounds of shells were higher. Every now and then she would holler for me to come and change the channel.

In hindsight, it's likely that she was depressed. My parents met in university in Egypt and moved to San Francisco together. The peace, love, hippie days of San Francisco of the 1960's was taking its toll on their marriage, so they moved to Vancouver, Canada—but their marriage still fell apart anyway.

She found herself alone in a new country with no support system and three children. She was desperately searching for community, a support network, and, unfortunately, this search led her to the local

Mosque. There she found that monster who offered to marry her, to make her whole, and to financially provide for her three children. She must have felt so alone, so abandoned. And without any belief that she had any agency as a woman, without any confidence that she could be a successful human being on her own, that she did not need a man. She saw herself as a parasite looking for a host. She clung to this man who was beneath her—as per the Egyptian class system—and who beat her children, but she felt like her only option was to shrug and accept what she could get.

In her depressed and confused state, the simplicity and order of Islam must have been so enticing. It offers a structure that is so rigid it outlines how you should cut your fingernails. There is a precise order in which to cut them, followed by a specific manner in which to dispose of the clippings. Nothing—no decisions—are left up to the individual. Every single aspect of your life is clarified for you. For someone who is scared and confused, such a system, designed with military precision, would be a saving grace.

She jumped in headfirst, akin to born-again Christians who "let go and let God," who proclaim "Jesus take the wheel." She didn't want to be responsible for making decisions. She wanted Allah to make all the decisions she felt unqualified to make. There is a lot of peace in that. She wouldn't have to weigh the myriad of options to determine the best course of action in any scenario; the work was already done. All she had to do was follow and obey. Walk along the straight and narrow path provided by the religion. What a literal godsend. She was intoxicated by the prospect. It allowed her to cope not only in a strange country with no support system, but with three noisy, needy children in tow as well.

She told me many times that she didn't like children. She would tell me how others would ooh and aah over babies and she found it so strange—she could not figure out what they were all excited about. A blob that drools and cries? But the culture she grew up in did not allow her the option of not having children—it was just what was expected. I never felt she actually wanted any of us, though, or even had a maternal bone in her entire body. Her culture also made it impossible for her to exert any power over her life. Quite often, unfortunately, in misogynistic societies, mothers are vicious to their daughters. Exerting power over their (female) children is the only domain where it is acceptable. Her disinterest in children, even her own, allowed her to drop my brother and sister off in Saudi Arabia to be raised by her in-laws who were expats there. My siblings were raised by our grandparents for two years. And then she got pregnant with me.

Apparently, in a desperate attempt to stop my dad from leaving her, my mom secretly stopped taking her birth control pills. When he was about to leave her, she told him she was pregnant again (with me), hoping it would prevent him from leaving her as it did before. But he didn't care this time. He still left her. I had failed to serve my sole purpose for being brought into this world. I was superfluous, useless, collateral damage.

Maybe after struggling in that marriage for ten years, my dad finally recognized that she was selfish and manipulative. Maybe he decided to save himself, so he went off, remarried, and had three new kids. And we were left to be raised by a narcissist who allowed a monster into our lives because it served her ends.

I used to dream that my dad would come and save me, but I never really knew him. My parents were divorced before my second birthday. Before remarrying and having three new kids, he used to come to visit periodically. He would take us to McDonald's and the aquarium. I remember going to his girlfriend's house and playing with her Russian dolls. But he was never a father to me. It was easy for my mom to make up stories about how evil he was because he was never there to defend himself. He was never there to prove her wrong. Throughout my life, I saw him, on average, about once every decade.

With no dad to save me, I used to imagine that I was adopted and that my real family was out there. I fit with them. I wasn't the black sheep of that family. Until we were reunited, I had no choice but to endure this horrible man that my mother had married who was becoming more and more a part of my life. I had to endure whatever aggressive, violent, or humiliating things he chose to do to me on any particular day.

One of the first things he did was break all of my mom's records and destroy our record player. He broke her Hank Williams, Dolly Parton, Fat Albert, and Kenny Rogers records with savage anger as we looked on confused. Why wasn't our mom stopping him? Why was she allowing this man to break her things? She stood sheepishly off to the side. She was so different when he was around. Suddenly, she was meek and quiet and incredibly accommodating. She was all I had to protect me, but she was nothing like Wonder Woman on TV. I understood in that moment that she would never stand up for me. She would never defend me from his beatings. She wouldn't even defend her records.

He encouraged us to get in on it, but I had no desire to destroy the albums. I didn't realize it then, but that was the very first coat of cement. It had not yet hardened, and so I didn't hesitate before questioning. I picked up the sharp, shattered pieces of Bill Cosby's stand-up album and asked my mom why he was doing this.

"Because these are all haram!"

Haram. How that word would grow to infuriate me! To this day, I have an issue with denying myself anything because of all the years I was denied practically everything.

EGYPT

Before you feel the heat of Cairo, you smell it—a dusty, faintly rotting, baked stone odour with a whiff of sewage. When I was in the middle of second grade, my mother moved us from Canada to Cairo, Egypt, without warning or preparation. In fact, I don't think she believed we needed to know. I think she just expected us to waddle behind her like little ducklings; eventually, we would figure out what was going on.

The best part, though, was that we were free of him, the "uncle." And I had escaped the terror of second grade—Mrs. Nyholt, who, legend had it, had once thrown a desk at a misbehaving boy. I had no issue with her, but I had been holding my breath because you never know what might set adults off.

Egypt turned out to be fun, mostly because I had a lot of cousins to play with. No one ever asked me to pray, and no one ever asked me to memorize any surahs. At night we would huddle together on the floor in makeshift sleeping bags made out of blankets. I only wet my blanket one night. After that, the embarrassment forced me to learn to control my bladder. I still sucked my thumb, though. After the lights went out, I would hide under the blanket, tuck my thumb in my mouth, and gently rock myself to sleep.

I awoke to the searing whine of the *adhan,* the call to prayer that is blasted from speakers atop Mosques all around, the last vestiges of the night's cool air—and the odour. Each building had its own personal landfill. Garbage was just thrown out the window down to a heap below on the street. Cockroaches and stray cats were as common as houseflies. We were living in the heart of Cairo, overpopulated, overheated, and overwhelming with its endless stench of either warm garbage, sewage, or both.

But I didn't mind any of that. The only annoyance were my constant stomach cramps.

My mom was less than sympathetic.

"Would you stop complaining? Every single day you whine about your stomach!"

So I kept it to myself. I kept it to myself for so long, I soon forgot what it was like not to be in pain. I now know that I picked up a stomach bug in Egypt and suffered from it daily. It went undiagnosed for over thirty years. Doctors in Canada never thought to look for this specific bacterium, because it's only found in people raised in developing countries. Well, Egypt in the early 80s definitely filled that bill.

It was a small price to pay, though. I would happily tolerate stomach cramps if I didn't have to see my "uncle's" ugly face. I was excited when I learned that we were going to live in Egypt—too far for my mother to call him over. I was overjoyed that I would never have to see him again.

I was fitted for a school uniform, and we bought books and pencils. I was worried about the language barrier and falling behind because I didn't speak Arabic as well as everyone else. I was worried that the school year had already begun months ago and that I would struggle to keep up. But my cousins assured me they would help me and that I had no need to worry.

As I was mentally preparing myself to join an Egyptian public school, it happened all over again. My mom decided to leave Egypt— no conversation, no explanation; suddenly we were on a plane back to Canada. I was beyond disappointed.

"But we sold all our furniture and our TV," I whined.

"We'll buy more." My mother was annoyed at having to respond to the interrogation of an insolent child. I was supposed to shut up and fall in line like my siblings.

"But where will we live?"

"We'll stay with Uncle Mounir until we find our own place."

My heart stopped.

"No! Mom! Please! No!" I screamed uncontrollably as tears cascaded down my face. To my surprise, my siblings actually joined in with my revolt. Normally, she would smack me down, but she was outnumbered this time, so she tried a new tactic.

"It's just for a little bit, I promise. We won't stay long."

"Promise?" We all pleaded desperately.

"Yes, don't worry. We will get our own place as soon as we can." My mother told me many, many lies over the years, but this one still hurts the most. I cannot understand, now that I'm a mother, how a woman could make a decision that terrified all three of her children so intensely. She knew we hated him and why. She knew she was lying to us. She just didn't care.

In Egypt, she had had the support of her sisters and her extended family. She wasn't alone. But they were all married, and she felt inferior. She could have saved us from Mounir's wrath. We could have stayed in Egypt. But she was divorced, and she saw herself as nothing if she wasn't attached to a man—even if that man was violent and would beat her children. So she preferred to make us all live in misery if it meant she could be attached to a man.

And so, we moved into his one-bedroom, partially finished basement in British Columbia, Canada. It didn't even look like a home. It was a weird mishmash of living room, dining room, bedroom, and storage area. Legally, he didn't have a permit to finish his basement, so we had to live in an unlivable space. The living arrangements were meant to underscore the hierarchy. Upstairs, Mounir lived with his real wife and his real children. As the second, inferior, illegal wife, my mother was relegated to the basement with her children.

While we were in Egypt, his three children arrived from Ontario. His oldest son was into hard drugs, and his ex-wife was worried he would be a bad influence for the other two children, so she had sent them all to live with their dad, and she moved to Egypt. Some people just keep having children and dropping them off here or there, as if they were things and not human beings. My mom dropped my brother and sister off in Saudi Arabia, my dad walked away from the three of us, my "uncle" walked away from his kids, and now his ex was walking away from their three children. I don't know how people can do that. But it seems to be a common story in my life.

His oldest son didn't last long. He ran away—got on a train back to Ontario. He got back in with his old crowd and shortly thereafter died of an overdose. I had only met him a few times, but it was enough to scare me away from drugs. The other two children, a daughter and a son, grew up with us. She was about twelve, and he was about nine.

The current wife (number one), a French-Canadian convert to Islam, was just as unhappy as I was with our living arrangement. I have no idea why she put up with it or how she could have agreed to her husband bringing in a second wife and her three children to live in their basement.

Her history explained only part of it. She'd grown up on a tiny island in Quebec in a Roman Catholic family. Having met other people from that same island, I have learned that it is like time stood still for them. Women there are still treated as subordinate there and feminism is a bad word. So she grew up in an environment where she learned that men were the masters and women their property; therefore, her transition to becoming a Muslim woman was just a short jaunt. She had had no romantic prospects, and her parents most likely thought she'd become a nun. As she prepared for her life in a convent, she worked as a nurse (not a real nurse, my mom was quick to point out, she "just cleaned bedpans"). She met a custodian at the hospital where she worked who was Egyptian and married with three children. They began an affair anyway. Who knows why—was he just excited to be getting "white meat?" Was she just excited to get the attention of a man—any man? Eventually, he left his first wife and his three children in Ontario and moved to BC with his new convert wife. This was around the same time that my dad left *his* wife and his three children in BC—us—and moved to Quebec. My mom really knew how to pick a winner!

So, the convert "won." He left his wife and three kids in Ontario and moved with her to British Columbia. She got her prize and was moving across the country with him. But things weren't working out as planned. She was able to get his first wife out of the picture, but now she not only had his three children, but a whole new (third) wife and her three children to contend with as well.

We took the brunt of her frustration. The washer and dryer were smack in the middle of the basement, and she would make a point of bursting in, swinging the door open with a bang, to do laundry, which I always thought was odd. Now I know she was just making sure we knew our place—nothing more than maggots in the basement.

For a long time, I repeatedly reminded my mom of her promise.

"You said we wouldn't stay long. You promised."

"Yes, soon."

Eventually, she got tired of the charade.

"Are you still stuck on that? Why are you still asking me that after all these years?"

Because I was stupid. Because I loved my mother unconditionally. And even though she gave me no reason to, I trusted her implicitly. I still hoped that her natural maternal instinct might suddenly kick in and she would decide to protect her children. Maybe it was because I had no choice. She was all I had.

HONOUR

With a house full of children, the three "parents" had to find a way to keep us all in line. We each had a schedule that we had to keep. We had weekly "family meetings" where we would have to answer for this or that. We would be lectured about some infraction, and then they would spend the rest of the time berating us about various things.

I hated those family meetings so much. What a farce! We weren't a family. When we were summoned, I would drag myself up the stairs, and then all five of us had to sit on the floor, as only the grown-ups could sit on the couches and chairs. As if the power differential were not made clear on a daily basis already, it was drilled home weekly. My butt cheeks would fall asleep, my back would hurt, and my neck would be sore from looking up at them.

Mounir usually led the meetings, but my mom would sometimes add some damning betrayal. If any of us missed a prayer, for example, she'd make sure to mention that. His wife was usually quiet unless she had something to say about his two remaining children who lived upstairs with her. She rarely talked about the three of us downstairs children. The meetings would invariably end with someone getting whipped. I suppose this was their version of Saudi Arabia's Chop-Chop Square. Their aim was to publicly humiliate the perpetrator.

After these meetings, we were sometimes sent away to check our schedules to see where we should be and what we should be doing. Other times the meetings ended with us having a meal together. His wife usually cooked because my mother was useless in the kitchen. Then the three girls would clean up. One of us would clear and wipe the table, another would wash the dishes, and the third would rinse. We were being trained to be good wives. Eventually, we were the ones who did the cooking, too. Later, in grade eight when I took cooking class in school, I aced it easily. I was a pro. I had been cooking for eight people every night for years by then.

It was only part of the training, though. To be a girl in a Muslim household has to be a fate worse than Hell. You are taught to be ashamed of everything you do, everything you are.

"Don't laugh like that. You're a girl!"

"Don't sit like that. You're a girl!"

"Lower your voice. You're a girl!"

"Lower your eyes. You're a girl!"

Girls are not ever allowed to look a man in the eyes. We have to keep our heads lowered like a dog to be reminded of our place as lesser than. It was endless. The word for *shame* was snapped at me in a loud whisper thousands of times throughout my childhood. "*Eib! Eib!*" It was the only word I heard more often than *haram*.

In whatever culture, if Islam is the dominant religion, there are variations of the word *eib* being spat at girls. Somali girls hear *ceeb* and *xixhood*; Turkish girls hear *ayip*; in Malay, girls hear *aib*; in Pakistan, girls hear *hiya*, etc. Girls are all hearing this because the family's honour lies with the girls in the family—specifically between the legs of the girls in the family.

Girls are how the level of a man's, or his family's, honour is measured. The more control he has over his wife and daughters, the more honourable he is. It is his responsibility to guard his family's honour by making sure the women in the family dress modestly by covering themselves up in hijab, and that they act honourably by keeping their voices low, keeping their eyes cast downward, by being demure. The most important aspect of honour is a girl's virginity. It must be guarded at all costs. Girls must not ride bikes, horses, or engage in sports lest the hymen break. Families must keep a close eye on girls making sure they do not demolish the family honour by losing their virginity—whether they do this willingly or because they were raped is irrelevant. The aim is to ensure, like a vitamin bottle, that their "seal" is not broken before they are delivered to their husbands.

If a woman dishonours her family by dressing too Western or not Islamically enough, or by having male friends, or by a plethora of other mundane things, she could pay for that rebellion with her life. Honour violence and honour killings are frightfully common in Muslim communities across the world. There are thousands of cases per year. And there is strong evidence that these crimes are underreported. Quite often, girls are reported as runaways or their families insist they committed suicide.

These cases are not limited to Muslim-majority countries. There have been cases of honour violence and honour killings all over Europe, an Egyptian man in Texas shot and killed his two daughters and in NY, a Pakistani man beheaded his wife. The stories are grisly and innumerable. Girls live in constant fear. The variations of the word *eib* are yelled at us to remind us that if we do not toe the line and guard our family's honour, we will be married off, or worse.

The boys in the family, however, were spared. They hardly ever got that word spat at them. The boys never helped with any domestic duties, either. I remember when I started refusing to do my brother's laundry. I was a teenager, and he was older than I was. He told on me, and it became a huge issue. I had to fight.

"He can't push buttons? His penis prevents him from knowing how to turn a dial?"

Predictably, I was the one who got in trouble for my language. I didn't care, though. I never did his laundry after that.

My sister, on the other hand, was a mindless drone. She did as she was told—even our brother's laundry. She never questioned a thing, never fought back, never even mumbled any annoyance under her breath. She fully embraced the role of sheep. Whereas I found the constant barrage of very specific rules to be constricting, she found it all so comforting and reassuring. She appreciated not having to think. She liked following the clearly laid out path. To her, it made life simple and easy. Sure, it was soulless and devoid of happiness, love, passion, and curiosity, but that meant it was also devoid of sadness, disappointment, confusion, and frustration. She was eager to trade in all the ups if it meant she could avoid the downs. She just wanted her life to putter along quietly until her death. Her main objective was to avoid burning in a pit of fire for eternity. She was not enticed by Heaven; she was terrified of Hell. That was the motivation. She was happy to follow the clear path to avoiding Hell. I was, of course, terrified of Hell too, but I was not as successful at turning off my brain. I was constantly and consistently pushing back or at least seething internally.

Because we were so different, I recognized from a young age that my sister was not my ally. If you said anything in front of her, she'd squirm—and you just knew she was going to tell on you. Even though my sister and our "uncle's" daughter were closer in age, his daughter and I were closer emotionally. We didn't fully trust each other, but we released slight frustrations intermittently by exchanging a glance or rolling our eyes. The parents were careful not to allow alliances between us, though. We were always pitted against each other. Oddly enough, their behaviour, as volatile and abusive as it was, was our only constant, and it kept us within their control.

SECRET SANTA

Iended up joining grade three late at the local elementary school, and because I had missed the end of grade two and the beginning of grade three, I struggled in math. I was able to catch up in all the other subjects, but because math is the kind of subject where the curriculum is scaffolded, I had holes in my math education.

I completed grade three and started grade four. It was in grade four that I finally started to feel comfortable in my new school. One of the cool girls invited me to take part in Secret Santa, and I was over the moon to be included with all her cool girlfriends.

I came home and told my mom the exciting news.

"I'm not buying anything for that *kafir* and her stupid *kafir* holiday," she said, briefly turning away from the TV screen.

"Can I bring something from home? Can we just buy wrapping paper?" I stood there, wringing my hands, hoping, hoping.

"Why are you such a *kafir* lover?" The words exploded out of her. "Do you know that it is haram to be friends with them? Do you want Allah to curse you? Allah does not love those who love his enemies." She turned back to her program.

My heart sank. I knew there was no way she would change her mind. Just once I wanted her to care about what was important to me. Just once I wanted her to put her religion aside. But I knew that would never happen. Her religion would always be paramount, regardless of what misery it demanded I endure.

I knew about the verses of the Quran that forbid Muslims to be friends with Jews and Christians or any nonbelievers. Quran 5:51 says "O believers, take not Jews and Christians as friends; they are friends of each other. Whoso of you makes them his friends is one of them. God guides not the people of the evildoers." What could be worse than Allah considering you to be one of the evildoers because you are friends with them? But still, I wanted to be friends with them.

On the days leading up to the day we would exchange presents, all my friends were talking about what they had bought. As the excitement built with them, I felt more and more sick at heart.

"That's because you're weak. If you were strong, you would go tell them that you want nothing to do with their *kafir* nonsense." My mother was impervious to my begging.

On the day of the exchange, I was in tears. I was mortified that my mother would do this to me. I would never ever recover from the embarrassment of being the only one without a gift for my friend.

Up until that moment, I had successfully sidestepped my way through the holidays. Around Easter, I dutifully painted the eggs in school and chatted nonchalantly about imaginary Easter egg hunts. During Halloween, I made up stories about my costume and all the candies I got. The previous Christmas, I even got away with listening to what the other kids listed as their gifts and repeated them when I was asked what I got.

"Oh, yeah, me too! Socks, pyjamas, a sweater . . ."

But the jig was up. I was a fraud. The truth was that Santa always ignored our house. I sat in the circle, holding the gorgeous plush kitten my friend got me, feeling like hot molten lava was churning in my stomach.

"It was so cute, I almost kept it for myself!" My friend giggled.

"You should, Cara! Keep it for yourself. It's okay," I pleaded.

"No, ha ha ha, of course not! I want what you got me!"

All eyes in the circle were on me as I explained that I wasn't allowed to buy her anything. That my mom wouldn't let me. Everyone was confused. They probably thought I was lying. It made no sense to them. They gave me advice that started with phrases like, "Well, why don't you just tell her . . ." or "How come you can't just . . ." Sweet, innocent little girls who had no idea what it was like to try and reason with a banshee. I smiled and nodded politely at their suggestions.

"Yeah, I'll try saying that," I said, knowing full well that I would never dare.

I truly appreciated that my friends were trying to help. I always loved my friends, even though they were *kuffar*. I knew I wasn't supposed to love them, but I did. How could I not? I was surrounded by kind, loving, and funny friends. I enjoyed being at school. I enjoyed being around them. I loved the carefree life of a non-Muslim. They didn't spend the day talking about all the bad things we might accidentally do that would land us in Hell. We talked about boys and Cabbage Patch Kids, and played games and read books! I read *Anne of Green Gables* and wished I could be adopted by a kind family far, far away.

But the word *free* was a dirty word. It was spit out with contempt.

"Oh, you want to be *free* like your *kafir* friends?"

Why, yes. Yes, I did. Freedom is a positive thing that is somehow twisted to be something evil. At school, I shed all my worries and stress. I lived my life happily. I never mentioned what my home life was like. I didn't want to think about it. I guess I was living somewhat of a double life. The real me was at school, the fake me—the me that swallowed all her unhappiness and anger because releasing it would only invite physical torture—that girl lived at home.

My mom was so hell-bent on minimizing interaction with our *kafir* classmates that she made us come home every day for lunch so we weren't socializing during the school day. I wasn't allowed to play with them at recess, either. But I always did. I felt guilty, but it didn't stop me.

ABUSE

Fourth grade was the year I told my mother that her "husband" was molesting me. I didn't have the vocabulary, but I told her what was going on. I had been taught to "always listen to grown-ups," especially a grown-up that would beat me if I didn't listen. So I never thought to question his actions. I was used to him hurting me physically—used to being forced to endure it—and not having my mother's protection. This just seemed like a continuation of the same. But there was something about the way he reacted to hearing someone in the hall that made me suspect he was doing something he knew was wrong. I wasn't sure, but I thought I would tell my mom just in case.

Her first reaction was to get angry at me and accuse me of instigating or inviting the abuse. I was confused at her line of questioning. It didn't make any sense to me. Her second reaction was to ignore me. I seemed to get a rise out of her when I first told her, so I continued to tell her, hoping to get that same rise again. Time after time, I would tell her exactly what he had done, how his wife was his co-conspirator, but she just continued to ignore me. She would let me talk. She would listen. But she wouldn't respond or react.

I was too young to understand what he was even doing or why, and I was too scared not to do exactly as I was told. One time he left me in his room as he went to his bathroom. He instructed me not to move. I lied down on my stomach and tearfully leaned down to the heating vent and whispered for my mom, terrified that he would hear me, hoping against hope that she might. But from the time I was five years old, she had never rescued me from him. Why did I think this time would be different?

My daydreams of being adopted or escaping turned to nightmares where I would stab him and slice off his penis, and I enjoyed it. The dreams terrorized me with their viciousness and brutality, but they also calmed me. I felt at peace watching his blood flow. Not a night passed that I wasn't haunted by those dreams. But how could someone feel so happy and serene at the sight of another person bleeding to death? I felt like a monster. I hated that I was so vicious, and I was angry at myself for feeling such relief wash over me as I had those wicked thoughts.

The statistics for how common this kind of abuse is in Muslim-majority countries is truly sickening. High-profile cases, like that of Zainab Ansari, a six-year-old girl in Pakistan whose body was dumped in a pile of garbage after she had been raped and murdered, have forced the international community to take notice. According to the Islamabad-based nongovernmental organization Sahil, an average of eleven cases of child sexual abuse are reported daily across Pakistan—daily. Zainab was among the dozen children who were murdered in Kasur District in Punjab Province in 2018.

What's even more harrowing than those numbers is the realization that most cases of child molestation are not ever reported. Mine wasn't. There is a shame, a stigma, a feeling that it is your fault or that you did something to cause it or that you could have stopped it. Girls could even be forced to marry their rapists in some countries. There are so many reasons that girls are scared into silence.

It is not just girls, either. In highly segregated Muslim societies, predators are not likely to have access to girls unless they have a daughter, but they have access to boys. In Afghanistan *bacha bazi* means "boy play," and it refers to a young boy who is being sexually exploited by men. In the 2003 novel *The Kite Runner* by Afghani American author Khaled Hosseini, the practice of *bacha bazi* is depicted. In the plot, the protagonist's half nephew is forced to become a dancing boy and sexual slave to a high-ranking official of the Taliban. The same official had, years earlier, raped the boy's father when he was a preteen and the official was a teenager.

The sexual exploitation of children is, unfortunately, sanctioned by Islam. Muhammed, the greatest example of humanity for all time, married a girl who was just six years old. For this reason, the practice of raping children is not taboo but actually revered—as long as the person is married to the child. Child marriage is therefore rampant in Muslim-majority countries. In Pakistan and Iran, calls to raise the legal age of marriage are shot down as un-Islamic. Nearly every two seconds a girl under eighteen is married. Some of those cases may be because the girl was raped. Many Muslim-majority countries have enacted the marry-your-rapist law, which stipulates that if a girl is raped, she must marry her rapist because no one else will want her. She is used goods, her seal has been broken.

It is important to remember that these ideas travel across borders. People with this mind-set do not magically change their minds when they move to another country. Girls all over the world are subjected to the same dehumanization, even if it is not the law in the new country they reside in. That is why it is essential for Western countries to protect their young girl citizens from the barbaric and archaic families and communities that engage in such atrocities.

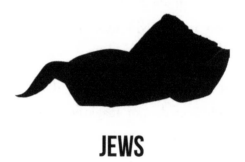

JEWS

My days began with being woken up before sunrise for the first prayer of the day by getting cold water thrown on my face. All the kids were woken up this way. I still have a fear of drowning.

Eyes stinging and head heavy, I would go through the mundane repetitions that robbed me of sleep. Afterward, there would still be hours left over before it was time to go to school. Those hours were spent reading the Quran. I would mindlessly moan out the foreign words that held no meaning to me, a rhythmic, hypnotic, nasal sound with a sinister meaning I learned many years later. I could barely see the words on the page through my tears and exhaustion. But misreading would result in a blow to the head, so I read and read and read. Rocking my body front to back, I mumbled the words aloud.

The point of reading wasn't to understand it; it was to memorize it. This is important. Muslims are not encouraged to learn or to understand what they are reading or reciting; they are celebrated for successfully regurgitating it. There are all sorts of perks and respect given to a *hafiz*, one who has memorized the Quran. There are no brownie points for understanding it. More often than not, those diligently moaning out the words have no clue what they are saying. The vast majority of Muslims do not understand Arabic.

It didn't matter what you were saying, anyway. As a Muslim, you had no choice but to accept it. There's no room for questioning or doubt. The Quran very clearly states: "This is the scripture whereof there is no doubt" (2:2). So what would be the point of reading it with an open, critical mind if you cannot doubt a word of it anyway? That's not even an option. If you are a Muslim, you swallow this book whole, as "the Fire whose fuel is men and stones . . . is prepared for those who reject faith." (2:24)

When I finally did learn what I was saying, that knowledge left a huge crack in the cement. I didn't even need to understand the meaning of it all. What I did understand was enough to cause fissures throughout the cement that was being poured on me daily.

I learned that for the past few years, nearly twenty times a day, I was referring to non-Muslims as the enemies of Allah. I was chanting that Muslims who became friends with non-Muslims were doomed to Hell, that non-Muslims were the vilest of animals, only fit to be used as fuel for the fires of Hell, that Jewish people were subhuman. Many verses accused non-Muslims of being liars who could not be trusted.

I felt duped, betrayed. I didn't want to say those things. I didn't believe those things! I had no idea that I had been mumbling hate speech every day. I loved my friends. In fact, they were the only positive things in my life.

According to Islam, only Muslims have value. It's okay to rape non-Muslims or take non-Muslims as slaves. All other people—other than devout Muslims—are to be met with varying degrees of hate. The most hated of all are the Jewish people. This cannot be overstated. The hatred for Jews in Islam is very clear, very deep, and unrelenting.

When I was in Egypt, I remember one of my aunts lamenting that the cucumbers in the market were smaller this year because the Jews were putting cancer in the vegetables. Even at seven years old I knew that was a ridiculous notion. You can't put cancer in vegetables. It should be noted that my aunt is not even that religious.

This is just the average speech of an average Muslim person. The only thing I can compare it to is the Communist boogeyman paranoia under McCarthy. But Muslims have been living with this paranoia for 1,400 years. Generation after generation, Muslim children are brainwashed to hate all Jewish people as Allah hates them, without rhyme or reason. Even Einstein couldn't escape this wrath. All of his contributions to science were dismissed with a swift "Einstein? He's nothing but a stupid, dirty Jew! What does he know?"

Since my father was Palestinian, he wanted to honour me by naming me *Philistine*, the name of Palestine in Arabic. But once my mother learned the meaning of the word in English, she changed it to a name that had a similar sound (in Arabic, my name is pronounced Yesmeen). Pro-Palestinian, anti-Israeli rhetoric was part of my life from the moment I was born. Hating Israel and all the Jews was a daily diet I consumed before I can remember; it was always just an accepted given. My mom forbade us to watch *Seinfeld* as it was all Jews. She would immediately hate a person if they had a Jewish-sounding name. The word *yahoodi* or Jew is used as a curse word reserved for the vilest of people. Among Muslims this hatred was generally blasé.

However, in the West, especially if you are a public Muslim, you have to temper your antisemitism. It has proven to be a difficult task for some Muslims in politics. The reason it's so difficult for them to know what is acceptable to tweet and what is not is that antisemitism surrounds them like water surrounds a fish. It is important to note that many Arabs and Muslims are not antisemitic, but unfortunately those people are silenced because they are not adhering to the accepted and dominant narrative. People like Bassem Eid get deplatformed or accused of being a traitor to their religion or race. Google *Muslim Zionist* and you'll find many people trying to get their voices out. It is unfortunate that rather than celebrate the voices of dissidents in their communities, people who risk their safety to call for love, acceptance, and harmony, the West props up Muslim antisemites who just fulfill the stereotype.

Many Palestinians in Gaza have protested against Hamas for its brutality and mismanagement of funds. Money meant to go to Palestinians instead goes to buying mansions for Hamas leaders or for buying missiles. Gazans protest by rioting in the streets and are gunned down unceremoniously. Their protests are barely covered by any media. No one cares. No one is interested in hearing about these courageous rebels that risk their lives to say they are sick of fighting. They want peace with Israel. They want a prosperous future for their children. But Hamas does not want peace. It wants to annihilate Israel and everyone in it. It is not ambiguous about this. This is clear to anyone who has witnessed any of the Al-Quds demonstrations that are held across the planet, even in Western countries, annually. Chanting hateful rhetoric in the streets is generally unacceptable in those Western countries, unless it is virulent antisemitism—that is ignored.

There is a prevalent impression that Islam is a religion of peace. Only people who have never cracked open a Quran can assert that. The Quran and Hadith are chock-full—*chock-full*—of violence. In the age of the Internet, there is no excuse for people to mindlessly repeat sound bites. Ignorance is now a choice.

It is true that although all Muslims believe the Quran is the literal word of Allah, not all are willing to act upon its demands. However, many are—enough to be featured as top trending stories on the Internet and TV because there is always a new event related to Islamic terrorists.

They say where there's smoke, there's fire. And there is so much smoke billowing from every corner of the globe, there can be no question that a huge fire is raging. At least five times a day over a billion people are droning on, calling for the death of all non-Muslims. This brainwashing undoubtedly infects many minds. Even if only 1% of the over billion people indoctrinated act on the demands, that is still 16 million people. And the truth is, unfortunately, that the number is a lot higher than 1%.

SUBMISSION II

Luckily, I wasn't one of the people who was successfully brainwashed. I just went through the motions and murmured the foreign sounds, unable to differentiate one word from another. I was an imposter in my own home. One time my mother saw that I had written my name *Jasmine* instead of *Yasmine*—just a direct translation of my name from Arabic to English. She lost her mind over it.

Her fake husband decided that this act of trying to be like the *kuffar* deserved the kind of punishment I would never forget—ironic, since he went by the name of Mike at work.

I sat staring at the wall, wishing I could disappear through a wardrobe to Narnia. I didn't even want to hazard a guess as to what diabolical plan he would come up with this time. Maybe I could find a secret garden. There had to be a way out of this life of hell. I just had to find it.

Before I could figure out how to escape, I heard my name being bellowed. He led me to the garage, where he tied my wrists together behind my back. I wasn't sure what was to become of me when he instructed me to lie down on the garage floor. He bound my ankles together with rope, a familiar feeling that brought up the familiar anxiety. I lay on that garage floor having what I now know was a panic attack. In that state, I was hung upside down from a hook that he used to hang the *Eid* lamb. He had devised a plan to hang me upside down like a dead animal. I swung back and forth as he stood on a chair to reach my feet so he could whip them.

Hanging like a lamb after slaughter, blood rushing to my head, snot and tears filling every cavity of my face, I discovered how to go into myself and somehow block out all physical feeling. I had read something about Shirley MacLaine invoking an out-of-body experience, and I had been trying to figure out how to do it. There was nothing I wanted more than to get out of this body, this life that I was stuck in.

I had plenty of opportunity to perfect my ability over the years, and I even surprised myself by how I was able to honestly and truly feel nothing. I would just cower into position and wait for it to be over. Unsatisfied because I wasn't screaming or running, he would turn his belt around so I would get hit with the buckle. More than once I watched him stare at me perplexed, beads of sweat pouring from his brow. I think he felt I was mocking his manly strength by not reacting, because it only enraged and encouraged him to continue beating me.

We would be at an impasse. Quite often I would let out some screams just so he could be satisfied and leave me alone.

There are parts of me (probably more than I'm willing to admit to myself) that are irreversibly damaged. It took me years to feel empathy as readily as I do now. When you block out physical sensation, you end up unwittingly blocking out emotional sensation as well. I'm not ticklish anymore. There's a photo that my dad took of me laughing as my siblings tickled me on the grass in Queen Elizabeth Park when I was about three or four. I look at that photo and try to remember what it felt like to be ticklish, what the joy of that laughter felt like. It's just gone.

As I hung in the garage, I was aware that I was upside down. I knew I was being whipped, but I felt nothing anymore. I pass out at some point, and the next thing I know my mother is screaming.

"What are we going to do?"

She was scared that he had killed me. She wasn't upset that I might be dead. She was only scared of what will become of them because they had killed me. As I came to, hearing her panicked screams, I wished I could just die. I didn't want to wake up. Why would I want to wake up?

I was so sad, so heartbroken, but I was still so desperate for her to love me. I was trapped in a dichotomy of yearning to be loved and accepted and appreciated by my mom, and equally desperate to get as far away as possible from her.

But I was unable to go anywhere; I had no choice but to play the part of the dutiful daughter. I knew my mother hated me. I knew she didn't care if I lived or died, and that was the most difficult part to deal with. I surmised that I was the reason she hated me. It was my own fault, because the devil, *Shaytan*, was so strong in me. I tried so hard to do everything she wanted.

What she wanted, it was clear, was to break me. She wanted me to stop fighting back and to just let the cement entomb me forever. Every single time I struggled I caused more cracks in the cement. Her goal was to make me stop struggling and just submit. This she hoped to achieve not only through the monotony of the five daily prayers, but by other methods as well. The aim was always the same: to teach us to follow without thought.

One common pastime was pulling weeds. No gloves, no tools. My calloused hands were dark with dirt that had been embedded into my skin. I picked weeds daily, a never-ending, Sisyphean task. I was confused—and furious—when I learned that there was such a thing as weed killer. Many years later, when I read the book *Holes* by Louis Sachar, I related to the plight of the characters. Digging holes mindlessly in the desert was meant to break the kids. I understood that.

Another task was collecting rocks. We would go out before dawn, after the prayers, and my siblings and I would fill bags and bags with rocks that we picked up from the beach. Sleep-deprived and with sore arms, we'd stumble into school with the other kids who had most likely spent their mornings having breakfast with their parents.

Another favourite was forcing us to eat "foods" like sheep intestines or cow tongue or testicles or the brains of different animals—for no other reason than to assert control. Do as you are told no matter how much you abhor it. Relent. Succumb. *Submit.* How could I possibly not hate my life?

The only thing I hated more was myself because despite the pulling of weeds and the picking of rocks, I was still alive in there. I was still fighting. I am very grateful now that that light never went out, although there were times when it was barely a flicker. If that light had gone out, I wouldn't be alive today.

I was taught that the light I clung to was actually the devil. Imagine being told that who you are is evil. What you love and connect with is evil. You try to change who you are. You try to be good and worthy of God's love, but you never can because you are evil. That constant struggle is debilitating. It crushes your soul and your will to live.

This is why ex-Muslims relate to people in the LGBT community so much, especially those who grew up in religious households. We know what it feels like to be told that the core of who you are is evil. Ex-Muslims use phrases like *in the closet* and *come out* because they are equally fitting. The plight of a Muslim gay person, a double whammy, has to be the worst possible scenario. A Muslim, gay woman—that has to be the worst fate possible.

I only had part of that equation to contend with. Although it was bad and made me dirty, I still liked boys. I had had my first crush in kindergarten. But with all of the competing things making me evil, this was the easiest one to push out of my mind. By this time, I was only in grade four, anyway, and boys were gross and had cooties.

With the eventual arrival of grade five came another change of school. But this time, the change was drastic.

Still living in his dank, ugly basement that wasn't legally fit for humans, my mother decided to enroll us in the newly opened Muslim School.

Calling it a school was a bit of an overstatement. It was really just a bunch of parents who had decided to pool their children into the Mosque's multipurpose room and take turns teaching different subjects. It was basically homeschooling but without any regulation or curriculum.

HIJAB

At the age of nine, I was fitted with my first hijab, which I was now required to wear. I hated it instantly. I hated it when my mom started wearing it, and I especially hated it now that I was expected to wear it. I begged for alternatives.

"Can I please just shave my head instead? What if I wear a wig?"

"Like the Jews! You want to be like the *yahood*?"

I tried to negotiate my way out.

"How come you didn't have to wear it when you were my age?"

"Because my parents didn't know better. They should have made me wear it."

I wished she didn't know better. I wished she would allow me the reprieve that she had been offered. I tried every tactic my nine-year-old brain could muster, but nothing worked. Gone were all my clothes; pants were no longer allowed. Now, I was to cover every inch of my body but my face and hands. This was the moment that the final nail was hammered into the coffin of my childhood.

I felt so awkward, so uncomfortable, so hot, in those stupid oversized clothes. My whole body was suffocating. My head throbbed, and my skin oozed sweat from every pore. And every day, they told me that dressing like the *kuffar* was evil and that I would go to hell if I dressed that way. Besides, when the Caliphate rises, if you're not wearing hijab, how will you be distinguished from the nonbelievers? If you look like them, you'll be killed like them.

Ah, the Caliphate. Always about the Caliphate. Every Friday *khutba* (sermon) there was the declaration that Muslims will succeed in turning the whole planet Islamic. Every Friday, we chant "Ameen" as the Imam makes a *dua*, plea to Allah, that the Caliphate rises soon and that we eradicate nonbelievers. Then there will be peace. It is why when ISIS rose in Iraq and Syria so many people from around the world-inexplicable people like university students from affluent families in Western countries-decided to join ISIS then burn their passports. The response from pundits was to assume that these people were all recruited online. That's some pretty quick recruiting! The reason why all those young and women so quickly joined ISIS was because, just like me, they were raised hearing about how it was their duty to join the *ummah* against the nonbelievers. They were taught that it was their duty to join the Caliphate when it rises.

Probably, like me, they didn't really think they would ever see the day, but then there it was. An Islamic State. As soon as it existed, these people already knew what they had to do. It had been drilled into them since childhood.

My mother used to sit me down and make me promise that I would be willing to kill nonbelievers when the time came.

"Yes, sure," I would respond in monotone.

There was always some sort of coercion going on. I was forced to pray, to memorize *Quran*, to promise to kill my friends, and of course to wear this hideous hijab. Every conceivable method of coercion was deployed—fear, a desire to please Allah, emotional blackmail. It was all unending. Only obedient Muslim daughters can go to Heaven. If you dress like the *kuffar*, you are choosing hell. That is the self-hate that I was filled with from the age of nine.

I was told of the Hadith where Prophet Mohammed claims he saw women hung by their hair in Hell with their brains boiling, because they did not cover their hair from men.

And I was told that it was for my own protection.

"If you had a diamond ring, would you wear it on your finger or would you keep it safe in a safety deposit box?

"I would wear it on my finger."

"No, that's stupid. Anyone can steal it! You have to protect it. Guard it against thieves."

"So what's the point of having a nice ring if you can't even wear it? What good is it in a box?"

"Stop arguing! This is better for you. You will learn to love it. When you grow up, you will understand."

"Can I wait until I grow up and understand first then, because I don't—"

"No! I have to do what's best for you even if you don't understand."

I never did understand. I wore hijab for almost twenty years, and I never understood. I went to visit my dad in Montreal in the summer between grades five and six. He didn't understand, either. He tried to get me to take it off, and I definitely wanted to, but I was scared that once we got back home, my brother would tell on me. So I wore a black cowboy hat that whole summer instead. My dad accepted it, as it wasn't that dreaded hijab, and technically my hair was covered, so my brother had no case.

Back home again, all the girls at the Muslim school wore hijab, too. And they all hated it as much as I did. It's true that misery loves company. The fact that all of us were forced to wear that piece of cloth on our head offered us all comfort. We all wore it, and sharing in our disdain for it brought us closer together.

And now, with social media, women across the planet who hate it— yet are still forced to wear it—can find comfort in each other. Under the hashtag #MyStealthyFreedom from Iran, there is a viral video of a seven year old girl crying and ripping the hijab off her head. She reminds me of myself, but I was not nearly as brave or defiant. She is angry because her parents tell her that she will not be allowed to go to school unless she wears this on her head. Her brother can wear whatever he wants, of course. Young girls or grown women from all across the world have posted pictures and videos under the hashtag #FreeFromHijab. A hashtag we created to give the women a place to find each other, find solidarity, find support...and, most importantly, to give them a voice—to expose this atrocity to the world.

It is important to clarify the distinction between culture and religion when talking about the hijab. A common response from people is that hijab is "cultural clothing." But which culture are they referring to? Women in Iran, Saudi Arabia, Somalia, and Indonesia share no cultural aspects. They do not have similar food or clothing or traditions or language. The only thing they share is religion. Hijab is worn by women in all those countries because of the religion of Islam, not because of any culture. Claiming the hijab is cultural clothing is as vacuous as claiming a Pope hat is cultural. Catholics from the Philippines, Italy, or South America share no cultural aspects—but they share a religion. There has been a deliberate conflation of religion and culture that only serves to erase cultures and replace them with the monolith of Islam. Dozens of countries lost their cultures to Islam. It is sad to see that there remains this pervasive idea that Muslims all share a culture. No. They do not. They each have distinct cultures that have just been shrouded by Islam in the same way each individual girl's personality gets shrouded by hijab so that they all start looking the same.

This erasure of individual culture is perpetuated by campaigns such as International World Hijab Day on February 1st—a day that is observed across the planet. On that day, Muslim women set up booths in places of business or schools and encourage non-Muslim women to wear hijab for a day. The direct response to that would be to have a day where we encouraged Muslim women to take off their hijab for a day, but of course we could not do that. Girls and women can be killed for removing their hijabs. Aqsa Parvez, a sixteen year old girl in Canada, was strangled to death by her father and brother with the hijab that she refused to wear.

So instead I deemed February 1 to be #NoHijabDay, and I encouraged everyone to stand in solidarity with women and girls across the world who do not want to wear a hijab but are forced to by their governments, their communities, or their families. The day was a heartwarming success! Women from Saudi Arabia and Yemen posted videos of themselves stepping on or burning their hijabs and niqabs (face covers). Women from Turkey started posting before and after photos of when they wore a hijab and after they removed it. Women in Iran, the bravest women of all, are imprisoned for decades for partaking in the #WhiteWednesdays campaign, where they wear a white hijab, or remove their hijabs, to show their resistance to the discriminatory laws.

Women all over the world are resisting. Women in Pakistan are riding their bikes in public. Women in Iran are dancing in the streets. Women in Saudi Arabia are wearing their abayas (the black cloaks they are forced to wear) inside out in an effort to recognize other dissidents when in public. And men are involved, too! Some men in Iran and, to a much lesser extent, in Saudi Arabia are joining in solidarity with the women protesting against the hijab laws.

Of course, all of these people are punished for their crimes against Sharia. Either they are punished by their families in what is referred to as honour violence or honour killings or they are punished by their governments that imprison them for decades for defying the laws created to maintain modesty.

Quite often I hear people wonder what's the big deal if you have to wear a scarf on your head? The big deal is that women are not even allowed agency over their own bodies! Hijab is just the tip of the iceberg. It is the physical representation of the subjugation and dehumanization and absolute gender apartheid that is commonplace in many parts of the Muslim-majority world.

While women in the West have gained their freedom to the extent that they are now calling to "free the nipple," women in many parts of the Islamic world just want to free their face and free their hair!

Women in the West generally support one another in their resistance, but it's important to note that in societies that are highly patriarchal and highly misogynist, women rarely support one another. Each woman is too concerned with saving her own skin to be concerned about any another woman's skin. This is by design, of course. If women are too busy viewing one another as competition—as their husbands can marry up to four women—then there is no threat that they will work together against the common enemy. Keep the women fighting one another so they are too busy to join forces against their oppressors.

The Internet is changing all that. It is monumental. Women are not only removing their hijabs in public, they are also dancing in public, singing in public, riding their bikes in public, jogging in public—all these simple activities are either against the law in some countries or come at a very high social cost.

MUSLIM SCHOOL

I didn't love the Muslim School by any stretch of the imagination, but I loved my friends. None of us bought into the baloney being shoved down our throats. We would hide out in the washrooms and sneak makeup on and tell one another stories about boys and the bittersweet excitement of getting our periods, which gave us a reprieve from the mind-numbing daily prayers. A woman on her period was impure, unfit to pray, touch the Quran, or even enter a Mosque. Allah makes you this way and then curses you for it. That's fair.

My mother was the Arabic and Islamic studies teacher there, so she was constantly stressing how important it was for us to behave and look the part of obedient children. At first, the other girls kept their distance from me. My mom was strict, and so I was regarded suspiciously. But soon they learned that I hated her as much as they did, and that we could all hate her together.

Because our camaraderie was so tight, my friends told me that a boy was saying that his mom had called my mom a whore. I tried to act nonchalant about it, but no matter how you feel about your mother, that's hard to hear.

"But your mom doesn't even know my mom," I said, confronting him.

"Yeah, when we were little, your mom tried to get my dad to marry her. She wanted to be his second wife! But my mom told my dad to get rid of the whore, or she would take the kids and leave him."

I denied any knowledge of the situation, but things were clicking. I had a vague memory of a large, sweaty, shirtless dark man. He would take my mom into a bedroom and shut the door behind them. I remember crying and banging on the door for her to come out. Every now and then she would emerge, in nothing but underwear, to tell me to shut up. I could never make sense of that memory. I asked her about it so many times. She always told me I was making things up or that it was a dream. But I knew it was real.

Despite this memory, I wanted to believe my mother when she said the whole thing was a lie. No one wants to believe their mom is a homewrecker, and even though I returned to school the next day to tell the boy he was mistaken, I had a nagging feeling that my mother was the real liar in this scenario. Like they always did, my mother's words managed to outweigh reality.

I know now that from the moment my dad left her, she was desperately trying to get herself attached to another man. She used the only commodity she had to offer. I'm not surprised she had such a low opinion of herself. She was raised in a misogynistic culture that taught her that her only worth was between her legs. She had never bothered to cultivate any part of her intellect or personality.

Someone that empty is the perfect raw material, the perfect vessel, to fill with religious fundamentalism. My mother was a stereotypical religious zealot. No sympathy, empathy or logic gets through to a zealot. There are no tactics or manoeuvres to get through to their human side. They are programmed to follow, and nothing interferes with that unbending single-minded goal.

The thing about her that scared me the most was that she could marry me off to an old man in Egypt. She threatened it constantly. I knew if she made that decision, I was a goner. There would be no recourse, no discussion. She would drag me to fulfill her wishes as she had dragged me, unwilling, countless times before.

Since the Muslim school only went to grade seven, all the boys were excited about starting high school, but the girls were terrified of what would become of them. The summer before high school was notoriously the time when girls disappeared. It was the perfect time to send them back home unnoticed. In the extreme cases, it was a popular time for so-called honour killings to take place. They are usually perpetrated in response to a girl being "too westernized." Much more common, however, was the threat of marriage. Every Muslim girl I have ever met is familiar with it: "I will send you home to be married!" This was much more than an empty threat to us. We knew it was a distinct possibility.

All of my fears were confirmed when my very best friend was sent to Fiji to be married off. I was scared for her and scared for myself. There was no email or social media back then. There was no lifeline, no way of contacting her. Once someone moved to a new country, they might as well have dropped off the face of the Earth.

BETRAYAL

Petrified that I would be sent away to be married, I continued to swallow all my questions and doubts and continued to play the role of the dutiful Muslim daughter. For grade eight, I was enrolled in the local public junior high. I found myself, yet again, having to make new friends in a new school environment. To make matters even more difficult, I walked into my first year of high school with a rag on my head. This wasn't like the Muslim School where everyone wore it, where it didn't affect anyone's judgment of me. This was different. No one would see me for who I was. All they would see was that odd piece of cloth. It would identify me. It would define me. And I was enraged about it. That was not who I was. That was not the image I wanted to project to the world.

I was determined to take on the challenge of pushing myself to shine through, despite the ugly cloth on my head. I made friends. I developed close relationships that filled me with happiness. And I appreciated my friendships even more, because I recognized that they were overlooking that cloth in order to get to know me. They didn't let that cloth be a barrier as it was meant to be. My friends didn't let it define who I was. They got to know me, and they accepted and loved me for who I was.

This was the exact opposite of what my mother thought would happen. I remember gleefully writing down the names of all of my friends. Since I had come from such a small Muslim school to a huge public high school, I was overwhelmed with how many friends I had! My mother asked me what I was doing, and when I told her, her face fell, blanched, and then pinched itself into an angry frown. She snatched the paper from my hands and read through it in a white-hot fury. I was way ahead of her—there were no boys' names on that sheet. I wasn't stupid.

But that wasn't her concern. She tore it up, enraged that I would be friends with so many nonbelievers. She had assumed that I would be a recluse, I suppose. She figured that the students would want nothing to do with the weird kid with the thing on her head. She thought she was safe sending me to a school full of *kuffar* because they would ostracize me anyway. Then I would be cured. They would hate me and reject me, and then I would have no other choice but to hate and reject them in return.

My mom's initial reaction was to try and take me out of school immediately. She threatened it, but she didn't do it. Instead, she told me to enjoy my final year in school, because I wouldn't return the following year. This terrified me. If I were taken out of this school—my only connection with the real world—I would never know happiness again. I was desperate. I was overcome with a sadness and fear that didn't even lift when I was in school. Usually, my personality shifted between home and school, between black and white; now I was just grey all the time.

My drama teacher, Mr. Fabbro, asked me if I was okay. His question reached me like a beacon of light in a deep, dark well. I was more than happy to tell him everything. I didn't hold back. I met with him and showed him the welts and bruises on my arms. In an Orwellian twist, a few days later, the asshole my mother had married stormed into my principal's office, angry that Mr. Fabbro had seen my arm. The audacity of him. How dare this male teacher see the welts and bruises that he had inflicted on this child! The greater problem here, he surmised, was that a man I was not married to saw my arm, not that he himself had beaten me.

As a teacher in a public school, it was Mr. Fabbro's legal duty to notify the authorities when a minor was in physical danger. Both police and social workers questioned me, and I told them all how my "uncle" would beat us mercilessly. I told them how he would walk in the door and—without provocation—grab me to release all his pent-up tensions of the day. He would pull off his belt and cover my body in welts. Even though I didn't feel them as they were being created, the bruises and scars remained as evidence of the beatings.

Mr. Fabbro warned me that if I went along with this, there was a possibility that I might end up in a foster home, that I might never see my family again. He asked if I was prepared for that. I was giddy with excitement. I was as light as air with the possibility that I would never have to see those people again. I was just hoping that sounding this alarm would prevent me from being taken out of school! *Am I okay with being taken out of that home?* I thought. *Are you kidding me? Nothing could possibly be more okay!* He also warned me that I had to stay strong, that I had to be willing to stand up in court and say everything to the judge that I had said to him. I always remembered my promise to him that I would stay strong. I envisioned myself courageously pointing him out in the courtroom as if I were in an episode of *Matlock*. I was prepared.

The investigation grew from interviews with just me at school to the police coming to the house and interviewing everyone else. My mother literally spat in my face and told me how much she hated me, but I stayed strong. I finally saw a bit of light glinting through the heavy layers of cement, and I was going to break free!

A part of me was surprised that she wasn't being more supportive. She had always acted like she had no control over him hitting us, like there was nothing she could do about it. Well, I was doing something about it! It was then that I fully realized she was lying and that she was actually just being manipulative. Of course, she knew what he was doing to us, but she pretended she had no idea and no control, because she didn't want us to hate her. It was our hate that she earnestly deserved, but she was a coward.

When she was questioned, she denied everything. She made me out to be a liar. My brother and my sister did the same. Mounir's two children also lied. Out of five children, I was the only one telling the truth. With their lies, they were all condemning me to this life. They were too scared of the consequences. It dawned on me that there was a real possibility I would never get out, that I wouldn't be put into foster care, that I would end up having to live there with them after I had just tried to have him arrested for child abuse. That was the scariest thought that had ever lived in my head.

The judge ruled that corporal punishment wasn't against the law in Canada, and due to our "culture," sometimes those punishments can be more severe than in the average Canadian household. The scariest thought crouching in the back of my mind became a reality with one swift smack of a judge's gavel. I never felt so betrayed in my life. It had been my only hope, and it had been dashed. How disgusting to allow a child to be beaten because her abuser happens to come from another country! What has that got to do with anything? All children should be protected. It doesn't hurt children any less physically, emotionally, or psychologically if they're from a different culture. Beatings and sexual abuse are equally damaging to all children, whatever their culture. If my abuser had been of German or Dutch descent, would he not be in prison? How does that make any sense?

These laws are still in place in Canada. I cannot even imagine how many children have been ignored or thrown back into the lion's den like I was. I have had so many people who were or are Child Protection Social Workers contact me to tell me how sorry they are. One man was so disturbed by the fact that he had to leave abused children to be abused that he had to switch to another role in the ministry. He just couldn't do it. He told me that he has been haunted by what he was forced to do for

31 years. People that have devoted their lives to protecting children are being forced to actively leave children to continue to be abused because their government is hell-bent on cultural and moral relativism. The need to seem woke supersedes the need to save actual children from abuse.

In their effort to be "culturally sensitive," my own country ended up being viciously bigoted toward me instead. I knew that if I had come from a family of "white" parents, I would have been protected. This is the typical result of regressive-left thinking, when their minds are so open, their brains fall out. They only see the skin colour or the ethnicity of the perpetrator, not the acts they commit.

If a white person refuses to bake a wedding cake for a gay couple, everyone will yell bigotry and assert that it is unacceptable. But when bakeries with Muslim owners refuse to bake cakes for a gay couple? The response is deafening silence. It's their culture, and we have to respect their beliefs—unless you're an Islamophobic bigot.

There is no greater stupidity or double standard today. We need to look at the action, the incident, not the skin colour or ethnicity or religion of the person performing the action. That is irrelevant. An immoral act is immoral regardless of who is doing it! We should all criticize bigotry, misogyny, child abuse, and other acts against humanity. Why do we care who is doing it? It's all equally wrong. It's the most heinous racism of low expectations if you do not hold all human beings to the same standards.

That was the first time in my life I had tried to stand on my own. I was strong. I was determined to look Mounir in the face in court, but I never got the chance. I had barely stood for a moment before my own country cut me off at the knees, forcing me back down to the ground.

It left me feeling like this was where I belonged, where I would stay forever. I was beyond devastated. I sincerely felt like it had been my only hope. I had nothing else to hope for, nothing else to live for.

I would be severely punished for betraying my own and going to the nonbelievers for help. It was the highest form of treason. I was taught that it was us vs them. And I just went to the enemy for help. It was unforgivable.

Islam has a very strong notion of fate. Everything is preordained. Any effort to try and create your own destiny is meaningless. What Allah wants will happen eventually. Your whole life is written before you take your first breath. This situation solidified those teachings. I wasn't in control or able to change my lot in life. I had to just accept that this was what Allah wanted. There was no sense continuing to fight.

My mother took me out of school at the end of that year, as promised, it was all for nothing. I just accepted it. I was numb to the world around me. If you take away people's sense of free will, then you take away any motivation for them to keep fighting. What's the point? They will never set goals to try and achieve anything because if it's meant to happen, it will happen. They just mindlessly move through the life that unfolds in front of them, never hoping or bothering to try to change their life.

Many years later—thirty years later, in fact—I reconnected with Mr. Fabbro. The moment I saw him, I burst into tears. He had no idea what had become of me. He assumed that I had been taken into a home. He could not believe that the court system had failed me. We spent the day in the restaurant where his son was executive chef, talking about everything.

He invited my husband and me back to his place, where we met his wife. She remembered those days so long ago, as well. It was like a dream sequence. I was overwhelmed and overjoyed to have him back in my life! I spent the next day crying as all the memories that had bubbled to the surface upon seeing him rushed back to the forefront of my mind. I cried for that little girl. Before I left his house, Mr. Fabbro said with conviction, "I would have taken you in."

"Yes, we would have," his wife agreed.

And my heart broke into a million pieces. How different my life could have been.

My mom did not allow me to return to school the following year. By the time I returned, Mr. Fabbro was gone. Our paths didn't cross again until I started writing this book.

MOTHERS

I spent my grade nine year following my mom around the Muslim School as her personal assistant. She had been promoted to the head of the Arabic and Islamic Studies Department. She finally had a role in society where she was being valued and revered. She took her job very seriously, and she fancied herself a pillar of the community. For a long while, this persona was solid. People bought into it, and they treated her with respect, honour, and fear.

The Muslim School kept getting bigger and bigger. Soon we had school buses bringing in children from miles away. We still didn't have a proper curriculum or classrooms or anything that identified it as a school. At some point, the government took notice, and suddenly the school was in danger of being shut down. Soon after, money flowed in from Saudi

Arabia. The money would allow for the construction of dedicated elementary and secondary school buildings equipped with the latest technologies available. Along with the Saudi money came the Saudi indoctrination. The fundamentalist Muslims that you've undoubtedly heard about—the ones blowing up buildings, burning school children alive, and throwing gay people off roofs. They are all of the same school of thought.

The old principal from India was relieved of his duties and an Egyptian man replaced him—an Egyptian man with a long beard and a wife who covered her whole body, even her face and hands, in black. It was the first time we had seen such a sight. Some kids called her a penguin or a bat, others called her a ninja.

My mom had an enemy now. A fellow Egyptian woman trying to swoop in and take her place as leader of the women in the community. People stopped asking my mom for advice, and they would go to the ninja instead. The ninja was considered more pious because she covered more of her body than my mom did. I couldn't care less about my mother's rivalry. She tried to get me involved, but I was a useless coconspirator. I had given up on life. I had nothing to give.

I had suicidal thoughts daily, but I didn't even have the energy to follow through. I was a shadow of a shell. I didn't even have any anger left. I drifted through the motions of life. Everything was colourless and flavourless. I had no desires, no aspirations, no thoughts or feelings. I just existed.

My mother, along with the help of the BC judicial system, had succeeded in breaking me, and she was smug about it. She would almost flaunt it as she commanded that I perform one demeaning task after another. I never resisted. I did as I was told. It took her ten years, but she finally got me to submit. In the morning, she would have me bow at her feet and kiss them. Then I would make her Twinning's loose leaf Earl Grey tea exactly as she specified. Anything less got me a mug to the head. One time the mug cracked on impact, and my eyes filled with blood as the wound gushed like a fountain. I pleaded for her to call 911, but she refused.

"Of course! So they can put me in jail, right? You think I don't know what you want? You want to try again?" she shrieked.

I was the enemy, and I was treated as such.

Daily, as I massaged her feet, she would tell me how I had ruined her life. How I wasn't supposed to be born. How she wished I'd never been born. How I brought her nothing but heartache. How my existence caused her nothing but misery. How she would never be able to be rid of me, either, because no man would ever take me off her hands. How I was fat and ugly and unworthy of anyone's love. It was an IV drip of poison that never slowed.

Many years later when I got involved in activism, I noticed a very common thread. A lot of us girls had been psychologically abused by our mothers. A woman who has no control over her life craves control. There are very few outlets where that control is acceptable. In her immediate family, she cannot exert control over her husband or her son, but her daughter is fair game. All of her aggressions and frustrations are released in that one direction.

Since, according to Hadith, Heaven is at the feet of mothers, mothers will get to determine if their children will burn in Hell for eternity or not. That is a lot of power to wield over a child. That power can have tragic results in the hands of an abusive mother. She can abuse the status and use it to control and manipulate. You must be an obedient slave to get her affection, support, approval, and, most importantly, to get into Heaven one day. She can revoke her "blessing" at any point, keeping you in line for perpetuity.

I recently watched a movie (that I related to so much) called *What Will People Say*. It is about a British Pakistani girl who was left in Pakistan against her will. She felt helpless and hopeless. There is a scene where she inexplicably violently abuses a cat. It is a short scene, but it is the kind that sears into your memory. In that scene, I saw a young girl who had absolutely no control over her life looking for an outlet. It was sick, heart-wrenching, raw, and real.

In our home, I was the cat. It was as if my mother took sadistic pleasure in torturing me. It satisfied some pathological need in her. And, unfortunately, she was not alone. In speaking with other ex-Muslim women, I discovered that this pattern of behaviour was remarkably common. Some Saudi Arabian women told me about how their mothers would lock them in a room for months. This is extraordinarily easy to do in a country like Saudi Arabia, where there is no protection for girls who are being abused. Another woman told me of how, after she escaped to the

United States and started dating an American man, she slipped and fell and started to bleed where she had scraped herself. Her boyfriend came running, and she flinched. She expected him to yell at her, to tell her how stupid she was, and ask her why she's so clumsy and why she can't walk straight. She was taken aback when his first words were, "Are you okay?" That was not the response she was accustomed to hearing.

I completely related to her story. I understood the level of abuse that no matter what you do, no matter what happens, you will be at fault and attacked for it.

Another woman, who goes by the name Sayeda Murtad on Twitter, recounted to me how her mother would exert sadistic control over her from the age of three or four. Her mother tried to get her to stop using her soother, but she wouldn't, so she put a hot pepper in her daughter's mouth. If Sayeda cried, her mother would shove her dirty slipper in her daughter's mouth. Regardless of the immeasurable pain she'd have to inflict on her daughter, she would control her. She would win.

This abuse with the intent to control escalated to throwing objects at her, strangling her—pushing her nails into her daughter's neck until she bled. She'd slap her, hold her by her hair and hit her head against the wall, hit her with sandals, with wooden spoons . . . she broke a rolling pin on her daughter's leg once and just laughed.

"That bitch doesn't feel anything," She had said about Sayeda.

Had Sayeda allowed herself to be controlled, as my sister had, it would have satisfied her mother's diabolical urges, but—like me—Sayeda fought back. And the fighting back is what drove our mothers even more wild. They only had one thing that they were able to exert control over, and they were failing.

Sayeda's mother hated her abusive husband, hated her life, and hated herself. She was full of pent-up anger, and Sayeda was her only outlet. She'd often tell Sayeda that she wished she'd aborted her. My mother often told me that she wished I were never born. For years, I agreed with her.

DEPRESSION I

Without warning, I was released from my mother's servitude to attend public school the following September. One day I was her drone, the next I was a high school student. It made little impact on me initially—my overarching memory of that time is of feeling empty.

Many years later I learned that my hero was a family friend who noticed how depressed I was—I suppose it was pretty evident, if not immediately obvious, to those closest to me. He had two daughters around my age, and he had watched us grow up together. He threatened to tell the authorities about my parents' illegal polygamy if they didn't allow me to go to school. There was a huge hullabaloo over this, and it caused the decades-long friendship between our families to be severed.

To this day, I have no idea why he did that for me. He never spoke to me about it. I barely spoke to him at all, as men and women were always segregated. My mother was as perplexed as I was. She expressed it with characteristic venom.

"Why would anyone care about you?" She looked at me with suspicion, squinting slightly. "How could anyone be willing to give up a friendship for *you*?"

The fact that her safety was being threatened—again, because of me—seemed to give her more reason to hate me. I was an unEarthly scourge that was the unending cause of trauma in her life. She never recognized or accepted her part in creating all these situations for herself. And so, under threat of legal ramifications, I was allowed to go back to public school in September.

That year, grade ten, was a tough one for me. The darkness that filled me was omnipresent. I made one friend, Amber. She and I would mope around singing sad Enya or Sinead O'Connor songs and getting lost in historical romance novels. I didn't actually enjoy the music or the books. I just followed along with whatever she wanted to do. I had no personal preferences or desires. I might have been released from the physical prison, but I was still imprisoned in my mind. There was no need to want anything as I would never get it anyway, so it was easier to just not want anything.

It had been two years since I had been betrayed by that judge, and I didn't even consider the possibility that I might ever heal. I just accepted my new, empty life. One day, I would be married off to some stranger, and we would make babies, and I would teach them to pray if they wanted to avoid burning in Hell.

That summer between grade ten and grade eleven, I took a handful of Tylenols, hoping to end my misery. I was really scared that I might actually die, as suicide was a direct path straight to Hell, so I thought I would "accidentally" take too many. But Allah can read your mind, so he'd know I actually wanted to take the pills. I was so confused and stuck. I hated my life, but I couldn't end it. Every path led to Hell, either on Earth or in the hereafter. But I took the pills anyway. If Allah wants me to live, I'll live—I'll leave it up to him.

Hours later, I woke up groggy and sweaty. I was disappointed that it hadn't worked. I wasn't sure whether to be relieved or not. I decided that one way or another, I had to figure out a way to get out of this darkness.

I found an old notebook with some leftover pages, and I started to write. I wrote out all the possible paths and all the barriers that restricted me. Eventually, after coming at my dilemma from every angle, I realized that the only way out of this was to just get through the next few years. Adulthood was a lifetime away, but it seemed to be the only light at the end of this tunnel.

To lull myself to sleep, instead of imagining myself cutting him open and spilling his blood, I would force myself to envision the home I would have one day. I would imagine walking in the front door; there were stairs to the right going up and a living room off to the left. When I turned to look into the living room, I saw the back of the couch and the TV facing me. I would always be sitting on that couch eating popcorn or ice cream. I would imagine getting up and walking to the kitchen. Sometimes, I would go up to my bedroom, and I would decorate it the same way every night, adding useless but pretty pillows and a throw blanket. There was a bay window in my bedroom, where I could sit and read a book in the sunlight shining into my room. I could hear children playing on the street below.

I never did get a chance to live alone, but those fantasies kept me alive, as I plowed through one day at a time, for years.

TIFFERS

As grade eleven started, I had no expectations. I assumed that joy was something other people felt, and I just accepted my fate: this is what Allah wants for me.

That was the year I met Tiffany. She helped me discover that a few warm embers still glowed in my internal fire. She enthusiastically threw lighter fluid on those small sparks and jolted me out of my grey depression. There is no way I can write about Tiffany without covering my keyboard in tears. I lost her a couple of years ago, and I will never be the same.

Although I had been an atheist for years by the time it happened, losing Tiffany was the very first time since leaving Islam that I wished I still believed in Heaven. To ease the pain momentarily, I would imagine that it was all true, that there was a Heaven and that I really would see

Tiffers again. But that's not how it worked in Islam, anyway. We would both be burning in Hell. I wanted to believe in the Christian ideal of Heaven, but as much as I wanted to believe, I knew it was all comforting lies. Tiffany would be the most disappointed in me. She would likely come back to haunt me to tell me how stupid I was being.

She was the first person to tell me that there was an option to not believe. I had no idea that was even a thing. She was curious after watching me pray, and she gently asked questions about why we did weird things like rest our hands on our knees as we knelt on the floor, then rhythmically lift only the index finger of the right hand up and down and up and down and up and down. You never realize how absurd something is until someone points it out.

"Why did your finger just have a spasm at the end there?"

"Oh, I don't know. That's just what you do."

"Why?"

"I have no idea."

"It's kind of weird, don't you think?"

"Yeah, I guess it is."

She changed my life. She opened my eyes. She awoke a spirit in me that was shriveled to almost nothing. For a person who was physically weak, she was actually the strongest woman to walk this planet. Tiffany had a congenital heart defect. Every year she lived was a miracle that perplexed her doctors to no end. But she was fearless. She was brave enough for the both of us, and then some. I remembered reading about Salman Rushdie, who secretly ate a ham sandwich when he was a child, then—realizing that nothing bad happened, he concluded that Islam was all lies. He was so courageous to do that on his own! But even with Tiffany as my surrogate strength, nudging me to do similar things, I was still too deeply indoctrinated.

"How about, just this once, you don't go into the bathroom with your left foot first and come out with your right foot. Let's see if anything happens."

"No, I can't. You don't understand . . ." This was why I didn't like to tell people about my life. Now I had to deal with this pressure.

"Okay, just humour me."

"Oh my god, no. I'm too scared." I wished I had just lied to her and not told her anything about my life.

"And don't mumble any prayers either. Just go into the goddamn bathroom, Yasmine. It's not hard."

"I'm gonna get possessed, and it's gonna be all your fault," I whined, only half joking. I was taught that people who entered the bathroom with the wrong foot or without reciting the short *dua* (prayer) would be possessed by the demons that live in the bathroom.

"You know how many shits I've taken in my life? Do I seem possessed to you? Do you think all these people who don't say a little prayer before going into the bathroom left foot first are possessed?"

"I don't know," I said. But I couldn't deny that she made a very valid point.

I cautiously entered the bathroom right foot first, scared stiff the whole time. Heart beating like a drum, I finished my business as quickly as possible and finally ran out, exhaling loudly.

"Are you possessed?"

"No."

"Okay, let's go get some lunch."

It seems so ridiculous to write these words now, now that I'm not brainwashed anymore. But Tiffers and I had multiple conversations that I am absolutely positive I would never have bothered to have with other people. She was so careful with me. I don't know how she did it. I would have walked away from this basket case girl and just joined some sane friends, but she stood by me. And she tried to get me to realize that there was something going on between my mother and my "uncle."

"No . . . no, he's just a family friend."

"A family friend that she's fucking."

"No, no . . . he's married."

"No woman would let a man do these things to her children unless she was getting something in return."

"No, Tiffers, trust me. It's not like that."

It never dawned on me how obvious it all was. I never suspected my mom of being a homewrecker, not once. I honestly believed all the lies she told me.

But Tiffany had planted the seeds of doubt. Seeds that took many more years to finally sprout.

After about a year of friendship with Tiffany, the cement had loosened to the point that I could wiggle my toes. Tiffany was my lifeline. I rode on the coattails of her strength and courage, but I was still not whole enough to walk on my own.

It should come as no surprise that Tiffany devoted her life to animals in shelters. Her home was filled with all the animals that she refused to let get euthanized. And once neither her home nor her garden could fit any more animals, she passed all sorts of misfit animals to family and friends. She had passion, patience, and an ability to rehabilitate abused and neglected animals. I might have been her first case.

Grade twelve, my final year of high school, was a bittersweet year. I knew it was my last chance at having a tenuous connection to reality. I knew that once school was over, I would likely be married off, an ever-looming threat. My mother had told me several times that once I finished school and was away from the clutches (and support) of my *kafir* friends, she would get rid of me. Tiffany offered to let me move in with her. They had a huge three-story house with a swimming pool that overlooked the ocean. But I couldn't take her up on the offer. I was sure it was just a polite gesture. No one could *really* want this piece of garbage living in their home. I tried to enjoy my final year as much as I could. I knew it would be my last taste of freedom.

That year, my real uncle came to visit us from New York, and he convinced my mom to move out of the basement. He admonished her for raising her children under such conditions. He helped us pack, and we finally moved out.

My mom always complained about how much everything cost and would threaten to move back again. I finally persuaded her to allow me to take a job answering phones at a pizza parlour to help out. I gave her all my cheques; I never kept a dime for myself. I was happy to be out of the house; that was more than enough payment. And if it helped to ensure we would never go back to living in that basement of horrors, I was happy to oblige.

Our rental home was a fair walk from the school, about fifteen minutes past Tiffany's house. So Tiffers and I would walk halfway home together, and then we would separate to walk the rest of the way on our own. On one of these walks she told me she'd heard a lyric that reminded her of me. She was hesitant to tell me lest it hurt my feelings, but eventually she let it spill. It was a line from Bette Midler's song "The Rose":

"It's the soul afraid of dying, that never learns to live."

Well, that just described me, if not every Muslim, in a nutshell. We were perpetually scared. Fear Allah. Fear Hell. Fear damnation. Fear the *kafir*. Fear the Jews. Fear the devil. Fear the Day of Judgment. Oy vey! It was never-ending. A constant fear spread like a cancer through my thoughts all the time, prohibiting me from doing anything, leaving me too scared to move.

And, no, we would never learn to live because that's not the goal. The goal is to die and that's when we start living. This life is but a test.

It's an illusion. Nothing matters. The *real* life that matters happens in the hereafter.

Every time I hear Bette Midler sing anything, I burst into tears. That was our song. Tiffers and I would sing it loudly to each other as we walked opposite ways home.

"Some say looooove . . ."

"It is a riiiiveeeeer . . ."

ABANDONED

As other graduates were chattering away about college, going away to university, or planning out their gap year, I answered all queries about my personal plans with "I don't know." Because I really didn't know. I had no idea what plans my mother had for me. I was never notified or consulted, but it wasn't like I had any say in the matter, anyway.

I was so afraid that this would be the end of my life. That I would never have a chance at life if I didn't seize it now. A friend asked if she could do my makeup and hair, and then we'd call up our friends and see if they recognized me. I was petrified, but I agreed. She did me all up and called our friends. Among them was a boy I'd had a crush on, but what was the point of even bothering to like a boy? It would only end in a dead end, in a pool of tears and heartbreak. So I never really allowed myself to even entertain my silly crush. But I watched extra carefully for his reaction. He acted cool in front of his friends, but he started to treat me differently after that. He'd find ways for us to be alone. We even almost kissed once in his car, but I was too scared to let it happen. What was the point? The school year was almost over. Why risk an eternity of torture in Hell in exchange for having a boyfriend for a few days?

I wanted to go to my prom very badly. I actually had plans for a friend to come and pick me up, but the night before, we went over to a family friend's house in a neighbouring city and had an "impromptu" sleepover that lasted two nights. I was heartbroken. My mother had ripped away my chance at having a happy ending to my time with my friends.

I have earned three university degrees since then. And I've missed out on each one of those ceremonies, too. What would be the point of walking across the stage if there was no one in the audience to care, to clap, no one to take my picture, to bring me flowers, to say congratulations. It would just have been a heartbreaking reminder that I was all alone in the world. So I never went to any of my convocation ceremonies.

After high school graduation, Tiffany went to Africa then to Europe, and I went with my family to Egypt for the second time in my life. In Egypt, everyone also kept asking me what my plans were, just like the high school friends I'd left behind in Canada, and again I would respond that I didn't know.

"What do you want to do?" It was such a silly—and commonly asked—question. What difference did it make? I never stopped to think about what I wanted. That would be absurd. Would you ask a slave where she was going to holiday that summer? I never even realized I had a choice. I would just have to wait and see like everyone else.

My (now married) sister was in university, and my brother was in college, so I asked my mom if I could go to college, too. She said, *Insha Allah*, which literally means "God willing," but realistically means *dream on*. She gave me no indication that I would be allowed to go to college, but she also gave me no inkling of what her plans for me actually were.

This time in Egypt wasn't nearly as fun as it was when I was seven. It was still hot and dirty. I barely understood the language. I knew I should feel some connection with the world around me, but I didn't. Nothing felt right to me. I was born and raised in Canada. Even though I attended Islamic schools, and my mother tried her hardest to raise me in a bubble, I was still Canadian. Egyptian culture was very different from what I was used to in Vancouver, and completely different from the way my mom had described it.

She always went on at length about how much better Egypt was and how much better Egyptians were, but I saw no evidence of this. Even her constant jabs at the *kafir* way of life were totally unwarranted. In this Muslim country, there were women not wearing hijab, Amr Diab dance music blaring all the time, parties where men and women were in mixed company. I even had the very first birthday cake of my life in Egypt. My eighteenth birthday was celebrated with an ice-cream cake, and all my cousins singing an odd rendition of "Happy Birthday" in their adorable, barely coherent accents. None of this was what I was used to. I found the customs confusing. I found the superstitions overwhelming. I couldn't make sense of the cultural norms.

I have an uncle who is a jinn hunter, basically like Sam and Dean Winchester in the television series *Supernatural*. People would contact him if they thought their house was possessed by a jinn (a supernatural spirit), if their child was acting strangely, or if they couldn't get pregnant—for all sorts of reasons. There was an earnest belief that jinn were everywhere. Jinn are mentioned in the Quran as spirits that live among us. Some of them wreak havoc and cause trouble. Others just hang out. Some fall in love with humans and act like stalkers. One woman felt her daughter had a jinn inside her that was preventing her from being impregnated by her husband because the jealous jinn was in love with her.

These were grown adults, educated people. They were successful in their lives and completely sane, but they believed this as strongly as you or I would believe that we need oxygen to survive. It was an unquestioned truth. Jinn possession and exorcisms are as common there as the common cold. Once you start to talk about your jinn story, everyone has a remedy for you.

"Oh yeah, my grandmother had that problem once. Turned out a jinn was possessing her."

I walked around feeling like there was something wrong with me. It never occurred to me that they were the ones with issues. But that all started to change. It was slowly dawning on me that adults could say, do or believe stupid things.

My uncle was eating a chocolate bar one day.

"I wonder what these crispy things in here are."

"That's puffed rice," I said.

"What?" He bellowed.

"It's puffed rice. Like Rice Krispies. Do you guys have Rice Krispies cereal in Egypt?"

"What are you talking about?" he scoffed. "Rice? I suppose there's also some vegetables and roasted chicken in here, too?" He was laughing so hard that he was barely able to chew his chocolate.

"Read the ingredients," I said.

"Don't be ridiculous."

"Read the ingredients!" I said again.

"Don't be stupid. I don't need to read the ingredients. I know it's not rice." He continued to laugh as he rolled his eyes and threw out the wrapper.

That is the mind-set of Muslims in a nutshell: I don't need to learn the truth—I already *know* it. I don't need to read the ingredients. I don't need to read science books. I don't need to learn anything more—I already *know*. And once you think you *know*, there's no desire to learn anything further.

One morning as I went to get dressed, I couldn't find my clothes anywhere. I kept them in a blue suitcase, but the suitcase was nowhere to be found. I started asking around. Eventually, I found the suitcase in the room my mother was staying in. I was relieved—now I could get dressed! But when I opened it up, nothing in it was mine.

"Where is all my stuff?" I asked my mom.

"I needed the suitcase."

"Ok, but where are all my clothes?"

"You don't have any clothes."

"What? Yes, I do. They were all in that suitcase!"

"I gave it all away to your cousins."

"Why? How? What am I supposed to wear?"

"You can buy new clothes. They all looked ugly on you, anyway. You are so fat, and you look horrible. I am embarrassed you're my daughter."

The tears just welled up. Tears of anger. Tears of confusion. Tears of humiliation. Tears of indignation. I started to argue back, but as usual, she would whip out the most vicious things to say to shut me up.

"I pissed you out. You hear me? You are my urine. You are nothing but my bodily waste! I excreted you! You are just a turd that I should have flushed! You have no right to question me. You are nothing."

I was not used to being treated like a human being by her. But even for her, this was an all-time low. I had no idea how to reconcile it.

"So we're going to go shopping for all new clothes that fit me when we get home to Canada?" I barely managed to steady my voice.

"Yeah, sure. *Insha Allah*. Get out of my face."

"What am I supposed to wear today? Or on the plane tomorrow?"

"I don't care. I said *get out!*"

I was so infuriated that my cousins came to me—sheepishly, embarrassed, apologizing—and tried to give me back my clothes. I took back a few favourites, but I left the rest. I would feel ugly and fat in them now, anyway, since my mother had poured vinegar on that old wound. I knew I just wouldn't feel the same wearing them again. Besides, I could go on a shopping spree when I returned home. I looked forward to that. But I was suspicious of her promise, since most of my clothes were hand-me-downs from my sister. I had very few that had been purchased just for me. So, I was hesitant to fully believe that all of a sudden, my mom would be willing to buy me a whole new wardrobe.

But what did it matter? We were leaving tomorrow. I couldn't wait to get back home and see Tiffany and hear all about her travels. Maybe I could push my mom to let me go to college. I could work to pay my tuition; she just had to agree to let me out the door. I went to bed that night exasperated, sad, excited, confused, and exhausted. It had been a whirlwind of a time in Egypt, and I was really looking forward to going home.

I woke up to a very quiet house the next morning. I thought it was strange that the sun was shining. *Oh my god! Did we miss our flight? We should have left for the airport hours ago!*

Heart racing, I darted around looking for my mom. I couldn't find her. The suitcases were gone. My sister was gone. My brother was gone. What was going on?

The familiar tightness in my chest, difficulty breathing, cold sweat, blurred vision—another panic attack was taking over.

I found my mom's twin sister. And even though I already knew the answer, I rained questions on her hysterically.

"Where is everyone? What's going on? Did they leave for the airport without me? Where is my family?"

"They left," she spat out.

DEPRESSION II

I had known depression before, but this darkness was particularly insidious. In the past, I had a reason to get up in the morning. Whether it was to follow my mom around the Muslim school or go to school myself, I was expected to be somewhere doing something. But here, in Egypt, there was no reason to get out of bed. So I didn't.

My mother had left me in the care of her twin sister. It was hard to tell which one of them was the evil twin. They were equally diabolical and manipulative.

The only good thing about Egypt was that Ramadan was less torturous as the days were shorter in Egypt. During the month of Ramadan, Muslims are not allowed to eat from sunrise to sunset. In Canada, I could end up fasting for around fifteen hours in the summers. And of course it was much easier when the whole country was in on it. No McDonald's commercials or people eating yummy-smelling foods around you.

For one month, the whole country shifted day and night. During the day, people would sleep, and once the sun set, they would eat, watch TV and movies, go out with friends, etc. It was a pretty festive time in Egypt because it wasn't all about starving yourself and reading the Quran like it had been for me growing up. Suddenly, Ramadan was more about the special foods, the music, and all the new television shows.

In Canada, my mom would just sleep the whole month away. We would watch the clock and then at sundown, we'd make a packet of Mr. Noodles or Kraft Dinner for ourselves. *Eid* was equally uneventful in Canada. There were no family and friend-filled feasts like they had in Egypt. In Egypt, families and neighbours would take turns cooking for one another so you wouldn't have to cook every day. Most of the month, you'd actually be going to someone's house for a huge iftar (breaking of the fast) spread.

Growing up, I was told that the purpose of Ramadan was to feel how poor people felt when they had no food. Naturally, my next question was why do poor people still have to fast? Don't they already know how it feels?

I never got a satisfactory response. I also asked why we wouldn't just give them food instead of depriving ourselves of food. Wouldn't that be more practical? But, again, no sufficient response.

I later learned that it was actually to train the *ummah* for battle. If you can go all day without eating, you'll be a much more efficient soldier. You'll be better prepared for the rigours of fighting a war, when the time comes that you are called to fight to support the establishment of a Caliphate. That's why most battles are in Ramadan. Well, that made a lot more sense.

My first few months in Egypt were spent aimlessly wasting away my days just eating and sleeping. I had no purpose and no connection to the outside world. I remember thinking that one day I will be old, and I will think back to all the things I should have done, and all the time I wasted, and I will be really resentful that all these days were squandered.

I had a balcony off my room, so that was the only fresh air I got. I would sit and watch the traffic below for as long as I could before the blistering heat, or the sand in my eyes, or the stench of sewage drove me back to my bed again. There was no email back then, no social media, no iPhones, no way of connecting to people far away. Even long distance calls couldn't be made from inside the house. You had to go to some phone place where you prepay then go into a cubicle and yell into a receiver so the person on the other line can hear you over the crowd surrounding you—not exactly the best way to communicate with friends back home. I felt completely isolated.

A beacon of hope shone for me when a neighbour told me about this newfangled device she had bought called a fax machine. I could fax letters to Tiffany! I was elated. I got deliriously excited as I watched her letters slowly appear from the machine. I had finally found a connection to the real world! I wrote her letters all the time. I had nothing else to do. Hers told me all about her adventures around the globe, and I lived vicariously through her once again. I, on the other hand, had no news to share. I did nothing all day. I just asked about her adventures and talked about how much I missed her and how I couldn't wait to see her again.

When I went down to the neighbour's to use her machine, I often bumped into her son. She had three boys, but this son always seemed to be around whenever I came over. We eventually struck up a friendship. He'd ask me about my life and why I was cooped up indoors all the time. It was nice that someone cared. He would ask me why I wasn't in Canada, and all sorts of other questions I couldn't answer.

My aunt discovered that we were talking, so she started to lock me in the apartment. Obviously, if a boy and girl are speaking together, it will lead to premarital sex, and then we'd all burn in Hell. So she locked me in that apartment as if I were a prisoner in a dungeon. Doors in Canada are made to lock people out, but doors in Egypt can lock people in, too.

My mother's nasty twin was preventing me from getting to the only thing keeping me alive—that fax machine. She had the similar uncanny ability, like my mother, of extinguishing any positive flame of hope that might start to burn within me. I hated her as much as I hated my mother, but I didn't fear her like I feared my mother, so I had that advantage.

I suspected that part of the reason she had such searing hate for me was because I told her that I would never marry her son. I shuddered, laughed, and gagged as I grimaced disgustedly and said that I would never marry my first cousin, let alone the child of my mother's twin! He was practically my brother! He was her only son, and from her perspective (where first cousin marriages are common) she took my disgust at the concept in general to be at her beloved son in particular. How could I, who was I, to refuse her little prince?

I had to devise a way to get out of that apartment and away from her. I decided to figure out a way to stay with a different aunt, my mother's youngest sister, as she was more normal. I spoke with my cousins about it, and they told me she would let me stay. The neighbour's son told me he would help me find a job. My plan was working. With everyone's help, I was going to get out of that house, get a job, and stop wasting my life away.

The next time we went to my youngest aunt's house for dinner, I refused to leave. My mother's twin pummelled me with closed fists—and she easily weighed over three hundred pounds. I didn't care. Unless she was willing to pick me up and carry me downstairs into the taxi, I. Was. Not. Leaving.

After repeatedly swearing and cursing and yelling, she finally gave up and left. My Aunt Iman took a risk defying her older sister, and she made room for me in her home. I was very grateful. I didn't have my own room anymore; I had to share a room with her two daughters, but I didn't mind. With my nasty aunt, I had had my own room, and all I ever felt was loneliness. I was happy to share the room with my little cousins. And even more so, I was happy to be free of that tyrannical witch.

FINDING MY FEET

For the very first time in my life, I had changed my destiny. I succeeded in altering the route that my life had taken. I didn't realize the significance in that moment, though. I didn't take the time to step back and recognize that I was actually in the driver's seat of my own life. I was happy, but all the credit went to Allah. I was grateful that he had let it happen.

I called up the neighbour's son and, as promised, he got me a job as a receptionist in his friend's company. Thank Allah that worked out as well! I worked with another woman who did all the actual work, as she was actually qualified. I just answered the phones to impress clients with my perfect English. I would meet clients and sit in on meetings for no other reason than to show off their employee who spoke English impeccably.

I worked there for few months, and in that time, I started to heal. My life to this point had seemed like a series of brutal smackdowns. I'd try to stand up as a kid, and I'd get forced back down. Eventually, I tried again as a teenager, and it happened again. After each blow, it would take less and less time for me to recover. I had been left stranded in Egypt for just over one year, and I was getting stronger.

I stood up tall and decided I was tired of taking the bus into work every day, getting harassed by what seemed like multitudes of disgusting men in that overcrowded country. No woman walking without a man was ever spared, no matter her age or how much of her body was covered up. It seemed like all the men fulfilled the stereotype: they took harassment of women as their civic duty. Research shows that whopping 99.3% of women in Egypt have reported being sexually harassed.

I decided to find a job within walking distance. There was a private international school not too far from my aunt's house, so I went in to talk to the principal. I told him I only had a high school education, but I wanted to teach English. He tried to hire me to teach in the higher grades, but I refused. I preferred to teach kindergarten, as I liked younger kids, and I was insecure about my (then nonexistent) teaching abilities. He finally relented but only if I would accept a pay cut. I made $100 a month to teach kindergarten full-time. And I was happy.

I started to find joy in life. I made friends with fellow teachers, and I started going out with them and living life like a real person. I would go to their houses, and we would go shopping together. We would hang out and talk about this one's fiancé and that one's boyfriend. My mother got wind of this and went into high gear to shut it down immediately. If I were left to gallivant around with other working women, I would be tainted and disgraced in no time.

"Are those women Muslim or Christian?" Her voice was scratchy and insistent.

"I don't know," I said, yelling over the background noise I competed with in the phone booth.

"Do they wear hijab?"

"No."

"Well, find out!"

"How am I supposed to find out?" I asked.

"Do they say, *Insha Allah*?"

"Yeah . . ."

"Well, you never know. Some of them think Allah means their Christian God, too. Say something about *sayyidina Muhammad* to know for sure. Next time you're with them, say *sully al nabi*" (bless the prophet).

"When would I ever have the opportunity to just yell that? And why would I? I don't care if they're Muslim or not."

"That's because you love the *kuffar*. If they don't respond with *alayhi salat wa salam*, that means they're not Muslim."

"Okay."

"If they are not Muslim, you are not allowed to be friends with them!"

I never did test their faith with the secret Muslim password. And my mom was losing patience with my newfound independence. There seemed to be no stopping me. She put a hijab on me, pulled me out of school, left me in a foreign country, but I kept being annoyingly resilient. My mother decided to resort to more stringent measures.

Since the campaign to marry my first cousin had failed, my mother and her family had now begun a new campaign to get me married to my second cousin. I was eighteen. I had no desire to get married. But my mother was adamant. She had left me in Egypt to get broken in. The plan was to tame me. Instead, I had successfully moved out from under the boot of her twin sister, and now I was working, earning money, becoming confident, stronger, and independent. Nothing was going as she had planned. She had to put an immediate stop to it. The pressure came not only from her, but also from my aunts, uncles, cousins, and even neighbours.

"What else are you going to do? You can't just work for the rest of your life! You have to get married," my cousins would insist.

As I mentioned before, the thing about being Muslim is that you are taught to ignore your gut feelings. Those feelings are usually attributed to the devil. It's the devil whispering in your ear and making you feel that way. So you learn to ignore your evil gut feelings and just do as you're told. You are told that those around you are smarter and more experienced than you. It's not like you trust your own ability to make decisions, anyway—it's a skill that is never encouraged or actively developed.

I accepted my *naseeb* (what Allah had planned for me) and I let myself get pulled into the whirlwind of wedding plans. I would choose the dress, the jewelry, the flowers, etc. I would play nice and do everything I was actually being coerced into doing. I had no interest or desire, but I didn't fight it. There were no alternatives. It was what was expected, and everyone was so happy. I quit my job—naturally.

One day on the phone, I asked my mom to send me a ticket to let me go home to say goodbye to Canada one last time.

"Oh, yeah, sure," she said, "so you can come here and not go back, right? Do you think I'm stupid? You're just trying to get out of that marriage."

I had never even thought of that. But it sounded like a great plan.

I would not ask again about going home. I would just gush about my fiancé and the wedding plans. She would be convinced that I was telling the truth because I would not give anyone any indication that I had any interest in going home.

Things started to get dicey when my fiancé asked me to choose an apartment with him. He was going to make a down payment to purchase a place that was way too big for a single man. I started to worry that if my plan worked and I went home, he would be stuck with this huge place. I warned him that he needed to choose his own apartment, because who knows what will happen between us—you never know what Allah has planned. What if he ends up with a new fiancée and she doesn't like my taste in apartments? I couldn't tell him that I was hoping to leave Egypt and never come back. I reasoned that there was nothing wrong with having a nice big apartment. It was too risky to tell him the truth.

We had the engagement and the party and everything. I wore a ring of fake flowers on top in my hijab, and I felt (and looked) like an idiot. No one had any clue about what I was planning. I had no idea if my plan would work or not, so I was carefully straddling the line between going home and staying in Egypt—just in case I couldn't get home.

But my plan, or rather her plan, did work. My mother agreed to send me a ticket to come home. I had succeeded in manipulating my mother as she had manipulated me countless times before. I had actually succeeded in changing my fate again. I had made a decision and had worked toward making it happen, and it happened. Maybe this is an actual thing, and not just a fluke!

Once I had the ticket in my hand, I told him. He wasn't a bad guy, but not a guy that I would ever be interested in, either. And I sure as heck was not going to marry my cousin. It was perfectly acceptable in Egypt—and all over the Muslim world. My brother almost married his first cousin. No one thinks anything of it. But I wasn't about to have a child with three eyeballs. I told him I was returning to Canada and needed him to keep it a secret. I told him that I didn't want him thinking he was being abandoned. I gave him back the *shabka*, which is jewelry that a groom buys for his bride, an Egyptian form of dowry.

"If you leave me, I will never marry another woman."

"Yes you will." I sighed. How could he be this dramatic when we barely knew each other?

"No. I won't. I will die alone, and it will be your fault. You will have to live with that guilt."

I apologized profusely and said goodbye. I felt guilty, but I wasn't going to let that deter me. I packed my bags with a spring in my step.

"Why are you taking everything? You'll only be gone for a month," my little cousin said.

"Oh no. I will never return to this place ever again."

"What? Really? Why? When will I see you again?"

"Oh, I might come back in ten years or something, but definitely not in a month!"

Again, I had to swear a cousin to secrecy. I didn't want anything to stop me from getting to the airport. I would lovingly fondle my ticket, reading the fine print over and over, memorizing the British Airways logo, reading and rereading the itinerary details. I was counting down the minutes.

HOME

When I finally got on that plane, I was floating on air! I had planned to tell my mother the same thing that I'd said to her equally nasty twin: "Unless you're planning on carrying me onto the plane back to Egypt, I'm not going anywhere!"

Once I got to Canada, I would get student loans and I would go to college and I would become a real kindergarten teacher! My future was bright, and I would not let anyone get in my way ever again!

When the plane landed, I scanned the crowd for my mom. I caught a glimpse of her and saw she had brought her fake husband to greet me at the airport. I felt like throwing up.

Once we got back to her apartment, I discovered that my "welcome home meal" was salmon. It was baked whole in the oven with the eyeballs intact. Disgusting. She knew I didn't even like fish. But it was his favourite food. She had likely used my return as an excuse to tear him away from his wife, and she was trying to win his approval. I don't know if he was more uncomfortable than I was, but it was certainly close.

I revelled in telling her that I wasn't going back to Egypt. I hadn't planned on saying anything until it was time to go back, but I was so angry that she had brought the man who had viciously abused me to the airport and then back to her apartment, I wanted to spit my victory in her face as soon as I could.

At first, she was flabbergasted.

"But the wedding! But the jewellery! But the apartment!" She was practically shrieking.

"I don't care about any of that," I said, looking her right in the eye. She changed gears immediately.

"I knew it," she said, her tone dark and malevolent. "I knew you were a sick devil child. I knew this was your plan! You are cursed. You will never go to Heaven without my permission! And I will make sure you burn in Hell for eternity. I always hated you. You are not welcome in my home! Get out of the house, you filthy cunt!"

"Well, I don't want to be here, either," I said, "but I have nowhere else to go." I was sick of her hatred and I was fighting back in a way she had not seen before. In Egypt, I was no one's daughter, and no one told me what to do. For the past year no one had yelled at me or insulted me. No one humiliated me. I'd had a taste of what it was like to be treated like a human being, and I was not about to give it up. But I was stuck here, living in my mother's home—at least for now.

Although my mother fought me every step of the way, I managed to get student loans and started taking courses at the local college. It was over two years since I'd left Canada, so all my high school friends had scattered their separate ways. I made new friends in college and even started working at the Dollar Store in the mall across the street from my campus.

Things were going pretty smoothly. I didn't have a long-range plan. I was just taking it day by day. I tried to ignore my mother's constant bellowing about how I was such a disappointment.

"What are you going to college for? You think you're going to move out and get a job and live by yourself like a whore?"

"I want to be a writer."

"You want to be a liar? You don't know lying is haram?"

"I said I want to be a *writer*."

"Yeah, so you're going to be a liar. Writers just tell stories. Are the stories true? No, of course not. They're all liars."

I tried, unsuccessfully, not to let it get to me. I eventually changed my major from creative writing to English literature to please her. Later, I changed it to English language when I decided that I would teach English instead. Being a teacher was an acceptable career for a Muslim woman.

I spent my days attending classes and hanging out with friends in between. One day in the cafeteria, a girl named Sarah told us a bit about her life. Her family was Muslim, so they always had these "strict" rules for her when it came to boys. I put *strict* in quotation marks because in comparison to my home life, hers wasn't strict at all. She told us she wanted to get a tattoo of a maple leaf because she was so grateful to be in Canada, and how she defied her parents all the time and was planning to run away with her boyfriend.

I envied her. I wished I could have had a boyfriend to run away with. I wanted to run away so badly, but I was too scared to do it on my own. The friends I made in college were all in the same boat as I was. One girl was from a strict Chinese family, and the other was from a strict Sikh family. We all connected in our mutual desire to get out of our current lives, but we were all too scared to do anything about it. None of us were allowed to go to the others' houses, so we all just hung around the mall in between or after classes. But we didn't push one another to run away—none of us really had the courage to, when it came right down to it.

I tried to reconnect with old friends who might help me get out. But it was hard to reconnect in those days. You had to hope their home number was the same, call up their parents and ask for their new contact info. Of course, the first person I called was Tiffany, but her parents told me she was living in Sweden with her boyfriend now. So I called my other close friends. One had moved to Vancouver Island with his girlfriend, and another was living in Montreal now. I couldn't find a lifeline anywhere.

One day I met up with an old high school friend. I was feeling particularly brave that day, so I told him that I had a crush on him. But he said he just wasn't attracted to me. *Of course, he doesn't find me physically attractive. And neither will anyone else.* We'd been good friends, but he was unwilling to look past my hideous physicality. And how would anyone see past this thing on my head to find me attractive and want to be with me if even one of my very good friends couldn't see past it?

Looking for a Prince Charming to support me in my quest to get out of my current situation was just not a realistic goal. No Prince Charming would be interested in this mess. I wasn't confident or brave enough to think that I could leave on my own. I couldn't see a way out of my current predicament.

The only consistency I had since arriving from Egypt was the perpetual bombardment from my mom urging me to stop embarrassing her and just get married already. I was now almost twenty years old, well past my expiration date, and this was just getting ridiculous.

"Who are you fooling by going to college? To what end? What's the point? Do you think you're just going to move out or work for a living? Stop this nonsense and just get married like a respectable woman!"

It was a daily ritual. And eventually, she wore me down. With nothing to pull me in another direction, I succumbed to her never-ending barrage of criticism. *It's true. Who am I fooling? What's my ultimate plan anyway? It's not like any normal boy is ever going to like me; I might as well agree to see the gross men she brings by.*

I met a few of them, and each was more hideous than the last. I couldn't stomach the idea of giving in, but I was also just tired of fighting. Truth was, I was exhausted. I still wanted my mom to love me. I still wanted her to be proud of me. And I wanted to have a smooth, calm life for a change. I wanted to quiet this constant pushing back that was happening in my heart, soul, and mind. What was I pushing back for anyway? What was my end goal? What I really wanted, more than anything, was to feel love and acceptance. And the only way to get that, it seemed, was to finally let go and just follow my mother's lead.

I decided to finally listen to her with an open heart. No more fighting back. I would follow along on her path and see where it led. Maybe I would find the peace and love I was craving so much. If I did everything she wanted, maybe she would finally not be disgusted when she looked at me. Maybe she would actually love me.

Maybe I would finally know what it felt like to be my sister.

My good big sister had dutifully married the son of the man who abused me as a child. I remember being beyond horrified and questioning my mother.

"It's none of your business who she marries."

"Did you tell her what her future father-in-law did to me?"

"I don't know what he did to you." Her denial was final.

Years later, after my sister had married him and had three children with him, after he cheated on her numerous times and eventually divorced her, she found me on Facebook, and I told her the truth.

"So, how come he never did it to me?" That was her response, to deny and deflect. I don't know why I was so hurt. I should have known. I felt like she had reached through the computer and stabbed me in the face and heart. All these years later, I finally had the courage to speak up, and she responded with that.

My sister was never the kind of person I would look up to, but she was the apple of my mother's eye. I wanted to know what that felt like.

My sister never fought my mom on anything; she always listened and followed her advice, regardless of how insane it was. After her episiotomy, my mother suggested that she sit in a bathtub full of saltwater, and she did it. I remember staring at her, wide-eyed, as she recounted the episode to me.

"You literally put salt on an open wound, Reema, how could you do that?"

"Mama said to."

"Yeah, but you had to know that was going to hurt."

"I thought it might, but mama knows best, so I thought I was wrong."

"How do you just blindly listen to her all the time?" I couldn't understand how someone with whom I shared the same genetic material could be so completely the opposite of me.

My sister never changed. She followed my mom, even though my mom's advice led her into black holes and misery. My mom convinced her to give up her children to their dad in the divorce because "no man would ever want a woman with three children." He took them and travelled across the planet to a Muslim country where he was free to have multiple wives.

The last time I saw my nieces, the youngest was four, and she and her sister were already wearing hijab.

But I didn't know any of that yet. All I knew was that my sister was the celebrated and beloved daughter, and I was the wretched annoyance. I decided to take a page from my sister's book and obey.

SUBMISSION III

Icontinued to meet suitor after suitor, refusing them all for one reason or another. I was willing to get married to make my mom happy, but I at least hoped to marry a decent person.

We were sitting with yet another suitor, for yet another meet and greet. I zoned out as he and my mom spoke in Arabic. I'd already made up my mind about not marrying a man who couldn't speak English, so I had mentally checked out. Another dud. As I was staring at the pattern on the rug, thinking about one of the assignments that I should be working on, I was taken aback as my mother leaped out of her seat.

"It's you! You're the one I have been looking for my whole life!"

I looked over at the guy, and he looked as surprised as I felt. I have no idea what he had said to get her all riled up, but she was clearly excited about this one.

Later, she tried her best to get me to agree to marry him, but I just kept refusing. I found him revolting.

"No. I won't. He doesn't even speak English!"

It got to the point where she threatened to kick me out, but I still didn't agree. So she tried another tactic.

"All my life, I have lived for you. I didn't get to live my life because I sacrificed my own life for your happiness. I could have left you all with your father and gotten remarried and enjoyed my life and forgotten all about you—like he did! But instead, I suffered as a single mother to three ungrateful children, alone in a strange country, all for you. All I ask is that you do this one thing for me, and you can't do it?"

The guilt trips and emotional blackmail were always more effective than the threats. I really wanted to make my mother happy. I thought that maybe this will be it. Maybe if I marry this guy, she will finally love me. Or at least she will finally stop hating me so much. I was softening, but I still couldn't bring myself to agree.

"Do it for me," she said. "I cannot marry him, but if you marry him and I live with you, then I will get to be with him."

That was a very odd thing to say, but I was still unused to seriously challenging her.

For months afterward, she continued to meet with him. I wasn't even there. She was supposedly vetting him for me.

"You're wasting your time. I won't marry him."

"I'm not wasting my time. I like to talk to him. You are so stupid. You don't know what a good man you are refusing. You will never find another man like him. I have lived. I know men! You know nothing. I am telling you; you will never find anyone this good, and you will regret defying me."

Those were some strong words. As a person who was never taught to value my own opinions, I found it very scary to be told that. I was sure that my mom did know more than I did, and I was terrified of making a mistake, but I still refused.

Her relentless pressure never let up. If I thought she was venomous before, she was an outright delicate rose compared to how she was now. She was absolutely ruthless for the next few months as she pressured me to marry this man. Added pressure was coming from him. He'd tell her of how he had a dream that I was reading the Quran to him and other signs that I should marry him.

She brought up every emotional blackmail card she had. She used every coercive tactic in her arsenal. She would refuse to respond when I spoke to her. She would even eat dinner out and not buy groceries. She ignored me completely unless it was to yell at me or spit at me for disappointing her and breaking her heart.

Islam teaches us that "Heaven is under the feet of your mother." If your mother does not approve, you won't go to Heaven. That statement ruled my life. I was petrified of her revoking my chances of going to Heaven—of her condemning me to an eternity of torture. She had the power to do that. To me, she was the physical manifestation of Allah.

The love/fear relationship I was supposed to have with him, I actually had with her. She held my hereafter in her hands.

"I promise you; you will burn in Hell for eternity. If you do not marry him, I will never let you set one foot in Heaven. You will never even smell the scent of the air from Heaven! I never want anything to do with you! You are not even allowed to go to my funeral! I will make sure that everyone knows that you are no longer my daughter."

That was her pièce de résistance her trump card. "You will never see Heaven. You will burn in Hell for eternity." How do you resist that kind of coercion?

My mom is a strange paradox. I used to call her the persecuted princess. She would manage to somehow be superior yet simultaneously the victim. It took me a long time to identify this dichotomy. I now recognize that she is not alone in this mind-set. I see a great number of Muslim people comfortably nestled in the same spot. In the news, you will see Muslims angry and confrontational about a Diet Coke or having to shake a hand or their right to cover their face during a citizenship ceremony.

Making demands on a country that you are not even a citizen of is presumptuous and condescending in the extreme. Yet, inexplicably, all of these situations are reported as cases of victimization. How does that happen? How can one simultaneously be the victim and yet exude an aura of superiority and bravado that surely undermines the claim to victimhood?

The weirdest thing is that they are successful. Because they have brown skin, they are automatically seen as a victimized minority. And they use that illogical white guilt to their advantage. A woman in Canada demanded the right to cover her face during her citizenship ceremony, though it was against the law. She eventually succeeded in changing our laws (before she was even a citizen). She knows she is not being victimized by Canada. She knows that she is being a bully. But she will play the victim if that works as a satisfactory means to an end.

Consider the group of Muslim protesters in the UK who were angry that the wife of a known terrorist was taken in by police for questioning. They chanted loudly and aggressively into megaphones: "UK go to Hell. British police go to Hell." They waved black flags and held signs that said *Shariah Law Is the Answer* and *UK Police Are Terrorists and Extremists*. After a woman in niqab finished chastising a British woman for walking in the streets "naked" (she was actually wearing a full-length dress), and asking her, "Who are you trying to seduce?" and telling her to "go put on some clothes," the protester then went on to explain that the demonstration was "a message to stop oppression." The irony would be laughable if it weren't so sad.

I don't know what brainwashing academy they all attended that taught them to use the same modus operandi, but I see clones of my mother all over the news these days. Christopher Hitchens called it the "horrible trio of self-hatred, self-righteousness, and self-pity." It was as if he'd been raised by Muslims. How did he hit the nail so squarely on the head like that?

I had the extra added bonus of being raised by someone who had the superiority that comes with being not only an Arabic speaker (Allah chose to reveal the Quran in Arabic as he loves Arabs the best. In the Quran, Allah states that he chose his prophet from the "best of people"

(Arabs). Prayers can only be performed in Arabic, facing Arabia etc.), but also my mother was of Egyptian descent. Egyptians fancy themselves and their country as the mother of the world. My mother had a god complex that rivaled that of Mohammed himself.

She continued a consistent stream of pressure that waffled between "woe is me, you don't want to see me happy" and "I hope you enjoy life in Hell because you will never see happiness." Inevitably, I grew tired of the constant pummelling. It was the opposite of what I wanted. I wanted peace. I wanted her love and acceptance. I assumed she would relent, but she never did, and the toxic home I was living in became unbearable. I just wanted her to stop hating me.

Through tears, I told her I give up. The tears did nothing to detract from her happiness. I had long ago given up hope that my mother would protect me, but this was a new low. This was a realization that my mother would actively put me in a situation that I dreaded in order to satisfy herself. She hugged me and told me I had finally made her proud and that she was so happy that I was making the right decision. I felt like throwing up. I was so despondent that she didn't even notice how miserable I was, much less care. All she saw was her own needs being met. But maybe now, finally, I would know what it felt like to be loved by a parent.

Almost immediately there was a *Katb El Kitab* (Islamic marriage ceremony). It is a binding agreement between the families of the bride and groom that the groom's family will provide a specific dowry amount, in my case, a Quran—I was assured that it was the most valuable gift he could give me. Neither he nor my mother acknowledged it was one of the millions of Saudi prints that were produced and distributed around the world for free.

Essam had agreed with my mother not to consummate the marriage until we were legally married according to Canadian law. The *Katb El Kitab* ceremony made it *halal* (permissible) for us to be alone in the same room.

He came over periodically for English lessons and tried to get me to give him a hand job or a blow job. But his requests were futile. I had no clue how to meet his demands—I'd never even kissed a man before.

He wasn't completely horrible during this "getting to know you" phase, however. He even called me on my birthday to commemorate the day—an act of rebellion, since birthdays are haram and should not be acknowledged.

I've often wondered why he was so restrained during this time. Was he fearful of breaking the terms of the contract he'd made with my mom? Was he afraid to risk her cancelling the marriage? Marrying me was his meal ticket, after all, his route to citizenship. Once it was official, of course, none of that mattered: he took me forcefully as was his right under Islamic law.

The Islamic ceremony was a strange and stupid "wedding." All the women were upstairs, all the men were downstairs; I never even saw the creature I was marrying. I just sat in the living room, robed in black from head to toe. The Imam asked the prescribed questions. My consent was not necessary—silence is consent according to Islamic law—and within minutes, I was his wife—his property.

Quite fittingly, months later in her fake husband's bedroom, where I had been coerced into vile situations as a child, I was coerced into a vile situation as an adult—the celebration of my marriage. I sat there as strange women did my hair and makeup. I kept crying and ruining their work, but they would just touch it up again. Not one heartless witch thought it strange that this young girl kept crying. Not one of them thought to say to my mom, "What are you doing?" Probably because they would all do the same to their own daughters in a heartbeat.

There was food but no music, because that's haram. There were no pictures being taken either, because the idiot I was about to marry believed that photographs were haram, too. Anything with faces is forbidden, even dolls.

Holding back the tears was proving too much. I had to let go. I had to release the pressure or I would end up in another full-on panic attack, and I had to avoid that at all costs. Panic attacks are too painful and too terrifying. Even though I knew my mom would be mad at me for embarrassing her, I let it all out. I heaved out all of the tears I had been holding back. The guests turned their backs on me. I suppose they felt awkward and uncomfortable seeing me sitting there crying like that, so they just ignored me and filled up their plates with more food. I sat there and stared at this surreal scene in front of me, trying to talk myself out of fainting.

Many years later, when the Internet became a thing, I came across countless pictures of Muslim brides crying at their weddings. As alone as I felt that day, I now know that I was not alone. I was joining the millions of girls before me and the millions of girls after me who were pressured into marriages they did not want. They are not tears of joy, as they would be at an average wedding in the West. They are tears of anguish, betrayal, and hopelessness.

This was very different from the forced marriage in Egypt that I'd avoided. Essam was not nice. He was foreboding and menacing. I never felt any positive energy around him. I just wanted to be as far away from him as possible. I was told he was five years older than me, but many years later, I learned from his Wikipedia page that he was actually fourteen years older! Yet another lie my mother had told me.

I tried to find optimistic reasons to accept my fate. I reminded myself that divorced women have a lot more freedom in the Islamic world. Once women are no longer virgins, no one cares about them anymore. They are used goods. So, I surmised, I would try to make the marriage work (and obviously it wouldn't, but then at least I could prove to my mom that I had tried), and after our divorce, she would leave me alone. I told myself that maybe I could even get a baby out of this. My very own little person to love and who would love me back. Finally.

I also learned later that these sentiments, these rationalizations that I convinced myself with, were extremely common. I met with and read about other women who had told themselves the exact same things when they were in the exact same situation. It's a sad bond to have with so many people. Each one of us felt so incredibly and completely alone, when the truth is that there are millions of us strewn all around the world.

The tradition of *Katb El Kitab* was started when Mohammed wanted to marry six-year-old Aisha. By agreement, she would be his according to Islamic Law, but he wouldn't consummate the marriage until the agreed upon date: the onset of menses. According to Hadith, that fateful day came when she was nine. It is not outside the realm of possibility for a girl to get her period at nine, but it is suspiciously young. The average age is twelve. Laughably, Islam apologists insist that girls mature faster in the desert, which is simply not true. Despite his conjured reputation of being the perfect example of a man for all humanity for all time, Mohammed's decision to rape a child has ruined the lives of millions, if not billions, of girls across this planet over the past fourteen hundred years.

My parents' engagement party (~1968)

When I was ticklish (~ 1977)

Happier days before showing hair and skin was forbidden (~1978) I'm the little one on the left.

I have decided to write a book.
it may be too late now since
Most of My life has already
passed. This book will be
written solely on Memories.
Let Me Introduce My self I won't
say My name for I hate it
with a passion, but If I havent
changed it by the time this
is published it will be on the
front cover. I am 14 years old
Its Christmas Time now, almost
the new year. Christmas has
no effect on my life for
I'm a Muslim (I'll explain
later right now I'm not in the
mood) Anyway Christmas doesn't
change me in any way at all.
I live With My Mother and My
_____ and Brother

A diary entry excerpt (~1988)

Before, when I used to hear about people wanting to commit suicide, I thought they were dumb, stupid and cowardly. I never thought I'd understand one day - like today.

I know, I know every cloud has a silver lining, but sometimes those clouds can get so damned black and the silver is hardly visible those are the times when I just give up hope.

I'm sure everyone at least once in their life felt like dieing. When your report card is full of fails, when you slip and fall in the middle of a crowd, when you find out a good friend may not be so good.

But when things come at a daily basis it really becomes unbearable and thats when people just have had enough and want out but there is no other way.

Well, I'm lucky I'm 15 (and a half) I have my whole and I mean whole life ahead of me I mean I haven't even been at the crossroads yet. I have a right to live, to live a good life and no one is going to change that or make me change that so my other choice is wait.

Wait, till I'm at the crossroads and choose my way. I'm sort of looking forward but I'm dreading it even more I'm a very hard person to understand.

Another diary entry excerpt (~1999)

With some high school with friends (Tiffany is to my left) (1992)

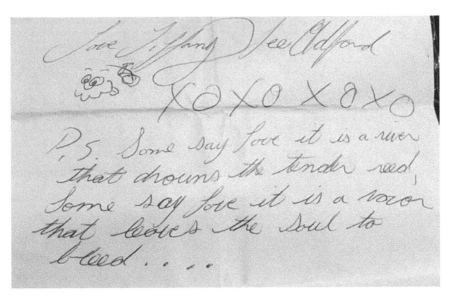

Excerpt from a letter from Tiffany, sent to me when I was stuck in Egypt (~1993)

Essam Marzouk, FBI photo (date unknown)

Essam Marzouk in an Egyptian prison (1997)

Me and Tosha (on my left) out clubbing with friends (2002)

Me and Tiffany, and our girls (2006)

Our wedding reception (2007)

We go all out for all the holidays that I was never allowed to celebrate
(Christmas 2012)

Dogs are considered dirty in Islam, but we love our little Norbert.

VIOLENCE II

Initially, the plan was for the three of us to move in together. That way my mom could live with this beast that she seemed so hell-bent on getting close to. But since it was difficult to find a place, we settled for two different apartments in the same building. My mother was on one of the lower floors, and the beast and I were on the seventeenth floor, the top floor.

Within the first week of our marriage, he came home to find the curtains wide open on a bright sunny day.

"Are you a whore?"

"What?" I had no idea what he was referring to.

"You want to the whole world to see you parading around here with your hair uncovered?"

"I haven't left this apartment all day."

"The windows! You don't think people can see you? Do you think it's only one way? Are you stupid? Walking around here like a stupid, naked whore."

"It's the seventeenth floor!" I finally understood his issue. "No one can see seventeen floors up and in! Are you worried about someone in a helicopter flying—"

And then he hit me. I wasn't completely surprised, as I'd become accustomed to being hit my whole life. It was more like disappointment, like *oh great, this again*. I didn't think that marrying him would be an escape from my abusive life, but it would have been a nice surprise.

"Oh, you just wait till I tell my mother!" I said. "This marriage is over. How dare you put your hand on me!" I packed a bag as I told him my plans to go down to my mother's apartment and never return. I was giddy with excitement on the elevator ride down. I had a great excuse! That was pretty easy. It only took him a week to mess up!

"So what?" she said nonchalantly. "Don't you know Allah has made it halal, permissible, for a man to beat his wife? You don't know your own Quran? How are you a Muslim and you don't know this? He has done nothing wrong."

"He's a lunatic! He thinks someone will be able to see me on the seventeenth floor without my hijab on! I am not going back up there ever again!"

"Oh yes you are. You have to. You can't stay here."

"Why are you doing this? Why won't you protect me?"

"Protect you from what? Your husband? You are *his*, he has every right to do whatever he wants with you."

"I don't care what his rights are. I am not living with him."

I stayed in my mother's apartment for days as she tried to mend the fences. There were no fences to mend. He refused to apologize because he was within his rights. My mother took his side entirely. According to the Quran, Surah 4:34, Allah instructed men to beat their "arrogant" or "disobedient" wives.

I was outnumbered and scared. How could I fight against clear directives from Allah? I still refused to go back upstairs, though.

"Okay," my mother said. Since her bullying tactic hadn't worked, she went with her tried and true emotional blackmail. "Just go live with him for a little while longer. If the marriage ends this early, everyone will think he divorced you because you weren't a virgin."

"I don't care what people think!"

"I do! I am respected in this community. Do you want to drag my name through the mud? Do you want me to be disgraced? After everything I did to reach my status in this community? Don't you know some people would love to have something bad to say about me? Just stay with him for a few months so that there is no suspicion."

And again, my mother's persistent coercion wore me down. Putting her needs before my own yet again, and with a broken heart, I reluctantly told myself I had no choice but to go back to living with that beast. I was terrified to go back. I might lose my opportunity to leave forever. I was terrified that this would be my last chance. I was terrified that I would get pregnant and then be forced to stay married to him. I told my mom all my fears.

"Don't worry, it will be fine. No one gets pregnant that quickly."

"Well, I won't let him near me. Just in case." I mumbled as the elevator doors closed behind me.

"You can't do that."

"What do you mean?"

"You are not allowed to refuse him. It's haram. You are his. If you refuse him, all the angels will curse you till morning."

I felt trapped in that elevator. Like there was no air left in the whole world. Everything about the laws of Islam are clearly arranged to entrap a woman in a forced marriage with a man who beats her and rapes her. All sanctioned by Allah.

It is incredibly common throughout the Muslim-majority world for women to be beaten by their husbands. It is so common, in fact, that in Morocco a popular daytime show had a segment on how women can apply makeup to cover their black eye. It is not against the law in most Islamic countries, because no human can forbid something that Allah has allowed. In Egypt there are debates on television where women try to say that men should not beat their wives, but they are quickly superseded by the Quran verse 4:34. Her argument is no longer valid. No human can contest the literal word of Allah. Some try to insist that Allah just meant lightly. Well, there is no trace of the word *lightly* in the verse. As well, *lightly* is highly subjective And finally, *no*. No one should be hitting their wife ever! But that argument will never hold any water in societies that have already accepted the opposite.

As well as being beaten, women are commonly attacked with acid in Pakistan and Iran for such infractions as dressing too Western, not wearing hijab, or cutting their hair. Women are not even afforded the basic freedom of choosing what to put on their body. They have no autonomy over themselves.

All of this stems from the edicts of honour culture. A culture that sanctions this control of women. A large part of this effort is to control women so they do not lose their virginity before they are given to their husbands.

After twenty years of guilt-ridden angst over impure thoughts, twenty years of "saving myself" for my husband, twenty years of buildup, the climax could not have been more anticlimactic. My first kiss was no beautiful, majestic Disney moment. It was forced and scary and gross. I did not like this man. I did not want him touching me, but my religion made it clear: I had no right to resist. A woman must not deny her husband even if she is atop a camel. I was sad and disappointed that this was the *naseeb* that had been written for me. I wished I had kissed my high school crush that day in his car. Then at least I would have experienced one decent kiss before I died. But I wasn't used to getting good things. Allah usually dealt me a rotten hand, so I was used to it. I didn't complain. I endured. This sacrifice would bring me closer to paradise and further from Hell.

Then the unthinkable happened: I got pregnant. I was stuck. But I was adept at resigning myself to just accept my fate, so I focused on how wonderful it would be to have a little baby to love, who would love me back. I hoped she'd be a girl. I knew I'd be a single mom one day, and it would just be easier to deal with a girl. Less of a mystery. My baby girl and I would be the best of friends.

The three of us moved into a town house, and my mom moved in with us. As soon as we arrived, he went around the house and taped brown meat-packing paper over all the windows to block out the sun and prevent anyone from accidentally seeing me. Then he covered the papered windows with a curtain just to be sure.

I never left the house anymore except for prenatal appointments. Those outings became my only opportunity to smell fresh air—well, as much air as you can smell through a piece of cloth covering your face. Once a month I would put on the ensemble that had come almost entirely from Saudi: thick black socks, a black abaya (cloak), a black hijab and a black niqab. The niqab was basically a square of black cloth that had two layers, one that covered everything but my eyes, and another, thinner one, that went over it to cover my eyes as well. The final part of the ensemble were black gloves. Once every single inch of skin was covered in black, I was ready to leave the house to visit my female doctor, with a male guardian of course.

And of course it had to be a female doctor; it was haram to speak to males unless absolutely imperative. "Like, for example, if a man is about to fall into a well, you can say 'be careful,' but not too loudly"—an actual verbatim quote from my mother, translated from Arabic.

I dreaded leaving the house. At home I could watch *Oprah* to connect with the world. Even though it was unidirectional, it felt like interaction. I connected with Oprah and her guests. It was inspiring and made me feel like I was part of the world. I was learning from them all.

But out in the real world, as I walked in the summer heat shrouded from head to toe in black, I felt the most disconnected. I thought the hijab was a difficult barrier, but the niqab was another thing entirely. If the hijab said "approach with caution," the full-face niqab said "fuck right off away from me."

Wearing a niqab you feel like you're in a portable sensory deprivation chamber. It impedes your ability to see, hear, touch, smell. I felt like I was slowly dying inside, slowly deteriorating. I was suffering both physically and emotionally. I wasn't allowed to have any friends, as no one was up to his religious standard. I didn't even know who I was anymore—if I even was somebody at all. My only actions were as a direct result of his. I would not dare to breathe unless he clarified in which direction to exhale. I'd say I walked on eggshells, but it would be more apt to say I stood tensely on eggshells, waiting to see in which direction I was to turn. He was a textbook abuser. I realized later that he followed the cycle described in my psych text like clockwork, as if he had studied it in school.

They were rare, but there were times when he made me feel like I was special. This was important, especially early on in the relationship, in order to hook me in.

"I don't want to go to work," he lamented one morning. "I don't want to leave you! I wish I could shrink you and put you in my pocket so you could be with me all day. This pocket," he said as he tapped his breast pocket. "So you can be close to my heart."

Those positive crumbs were far outweighed by the famine in between, but I lived for the next feast. The next time he'd be kind or thoughtful or even just not cruel.

To complete the cycle, and in order to completely submerge me under his abusive spell, he would use classical conditioning. A fist to my face replaced Pavlov's dinner bell. I thought everything was haram before, but I had no idea how many more things could be haram.

One time I was looking up something in the phone book and absentmindedly began to sing:

"A B C D E F G . . . H I J—"

"What the hell are you doing?" he bellowed. The back of his hand hit my mouth.

This was another one of those moments when I was just at a loss. What exactly had I done? What was my transgression this time?

"Why are you singing in my house? Are you trying to bring the devil in here?"

"It's in alphabetical order. I was just—"

"I don't care about your stupid excuses!"

Up until then I thought singing was okay and only music was haram, but nope—turns out singing the alphabet to help you look up something in alphabetical order conjures the devil.

As my belly grew, so did the constant beatings. I was so scared of him that I avoided him as much as possible. Even if he were in the bathroom, I wouldn't knock on the door because I didn't want to interact with him. I never knew where the land mines were. I never knew what would trigger a beating. At my lowest point, as he dawdled in the bathroom and as my pregnant belly pushed on my bladder, I rolled up a bath towel from the laundry basket and sat on it to relieve myself. I chose to pee on myself rather than to speak to him.

Though I never knew what would set him off, most of the beatings were over food. Those years caused me so much anxiety around food that over a decade later, married to a man I love, I still could not cook for him. Those years caused me to hate cooking so much that the mere thought of preparing a meal for someone filled me with a sense of panic and dread. I eventually got over the anxiety of cooking in general, but I still will not cook any Arabic foods.

Back then, my days revolved around making meals just so. That entirely filled the day. He would buy cookbooks and leave sticky notes on the pictures that he liked, and I had to create those dishes. Of course, the dishes I made never matched the photographs to his liking, so the common response would be to throw his plate at me.

On the days he did eat the food I had prepared, he would give me a detailed rundown of how it could be improved for next time. He was very specific with his demands. It was obsessive. He didn't like casseroles or anything in a sauce. He only liked finger foods or appetizers. This, of course, meant that whatever thing he ordered would be tedious to make, as they would need to be created individually. One time when I was speaking to a friend on the phone, she asked me why I sounded so sad.

"He's pissed off at the dinner I made."

"What did you make?"

"Roast chicken, rice, and salad."

"That sounds wonderful!" she said. Being a university student, her meals usually came in a packet.

She's right. He should be grateful that he has a good meal in front of him! Fucker. I tried to reach him from an Islamic perspective. I told him that he should be grateful for what he has, for what I had made for him. But I ended up with a bruised face because he took my words to be demeaning. He said I was accusing him of being weak in religion, a bad Muslim.

I asked my mom for this big plaque she had in her apartment that said, *alhamdu lillah* (thanks be to Allah). I hung it up on the wall right in front of his face where he sat to eat dinner. If I couldn't talk to him about it, I would try to send him this subliminal message instead.

I also tried to introduce him to "exotic" Canadian foods. I hoped he would be sold on the novelty of it, and, of course, they'd be a billion times easier to make than Middle Eastern foods. He never did like Canadian food, but, periodically, I would try to slip a dish in.

One night as I was preparing the "ancient Canadian delicacy" called chicken noodle soup, I realized that he would be home soon, and I still had a lot to do. I was busy separating the boiled chicken from the bone and the cartilage and skin and everything else. I had to make sure I didn't add anything but the purest chicken meat to his soup. Even the bits of chicken that were too dark would send him into a rage. I was scared to rush through the process, but I still had to clean up the house, shower, and get dressed.

Timidly, I asked my mother for help.

"Please be careful. Only put the cleanest bits of meat. I've already chopped up the breast, so if you can't get a lot, don't worry. You know how he is, if the first thing he sees isn't meat, he loses his mind. Just add the chicken to this pot."

"Okay, okay. I'm not stupid. Just go."

"I know, but please be careful. Actually, forget it, there's enough chicken in it already." I was too nervous to leave her with this task. Messing up his food always came with dire consequences.

"I said I know. Just go clean yourself up before your husband sees you like that."

I was nervous to walk away. I had never trusted my mother to help with any meals before, but I was too strapped for time, and every simple task is magnified when you're pregnant, so I left her to finish the soup and waddled away.

Later, as he sat down to dinner, I dipped the ladle into the pot to serve him his soup. As I lifted it up out of the broth, I was completely stunned to see that the ladle in my hand was filled with chicken bones, fat, and skin. I dropped it quickly before he could catch a glimpse.

"What's taking you so long?"

"I . . ." My brain wasn't connecting.

"Why is she so stupid?" he asked my mom.

My mom giggled in response.

I dipped the ladle in again. And I was met with the same mix of chicken carcass waste. I wasn't sure how all that garbage could possibly have got in there by accident. It wasn't just a bone or two. It was as if the strainer full of the discarded chicken bits had been dumped directly into the pot.

He was getting impatient.

"I've been working all day!" he yelled. "Can't you even get a decent motherfucking meal on the table on time? You sit at home doing nothing all day!"

I glanced over to the strainer that used to be full of bones and other waste; it was empty. Shocked, my eyes quickly darted to my mother. She seemed to be too interested in the pattern on the tablecloth to meet my eyes.

"What is wrong with you?" He jumped out of his seat and was standing beside me in one leap. "Serve the fucking soup!"

I had no choice but to dip the ladle in again as he watched me. It emerged as it had twice before.

"What is this?" he whispered menacingly.

"I . . . er . . . had so much to do. This pregnancy makes me tired. I asked Mom to help with the chicken."

"What? You're going to try to blame this on me?"

Blame what? How would she know what I was going to say? She was still sitting at the table. How could she see what was in that ladle? Up until that moment, I had thought it was an honest mistake. I wasn't sure how she could possibly have dumped all that in by accident, but I just couldn't fathom the alternative. Now, I had no choice but to see the truth.

All those years of making excuses for her. Thinking I misunderstood. Accepting her rationales. Continuing to give her my trust. Continuing to vie for her love. Blaming myself. Hating myself. Accepting that I was a failure. Struggling to appease her. Putting her wants and needs before my own. It all came crashing down in this one clear incident that I had absolutely no way of denying. I looked up at him, expecting him to finish me off. But no physical blow could compare to the inner pain I was feeling.

And then, the weirdest thing happened. He said, "It's okay. Let's just skip the soup. What else is for dinner?"

He took pity on me. He knew that my mother had done this. He understood that she had fucked me over. He saw in my eyes that I knew, too. He knew her hope was to witness yet another beating. And as I would scream for her, as he pulled my hair and punched my face, she would say, as she always did: "Shut up! The neighbours will hear you! Do you want him to go to prison?"

This evil man, who I would later learn was involved in bombings that killed hundreds of people, a man who had been involved in the largest terrorist court case in Egyptian history—second only to the court case around the assassination of President Anwar Sadat—had more of a heart than my own mother.

MY BABY

I knew my mother was vile and evil, but I needed her. I had just passed my twenty-second birthday, and now I was responsible for a new life. I was barely able to care for myself, let alone someone else. I was scared. I was nervous. I was overcome with love for my little baby, but in almost equal amount I was overcome with this heavy sense of responsibility. I loved babies, but when they'd cry, I'd hand them over to their mother. Now this baby was being handed over to *me*. How was I supposed to know what to do?

The only other baby I had been responsible for was my nephew when my sister was in hospital having more babies.

"Ooh" my mother had cooed as she changed his diaper. "Look how big he is. Like his grandfather!"

"Which one?" my sister responded wryly. The room fell silent as it dawned on me that my mother had slept with both of his grandfathers.

"Ew." I breathed out almost inaudibly.

As imperfect as my mother was, she was the only person that could help me care for my newborn. She was the only person in the hospital with me when I gave birth. As imperfect a mother as she was, she still knew more than I did. I had no idea how to care for this tiny, fragile life.

A few days after my baby was born, I got a phone call from a nurse. It was a service provided by the government for new mothers.

"How is she sleeping?" she asked.

"Really well. She sleeps all night and a lot during the day, too."

"How is she eating?"

"Hardly at all. She's always so sleepy."

"Oh. Does she cry a lot?" the nurse asked after a slight pause.

"No, not at all. She's content to swing in her swing. She's a really good baby."

"I would like to come visit you, but I can't today, so I need you to do something for me. Look at the whites of her eyes and tell me if they're yellow."

"Is she okay? She's just a good baby. My mom said they're supposed to sleep this much."

"No. She should be feeding every couple of hours, Yasmine. She's not eating enough."

I turned to check on her dozing in the crib next to me. She *did* sleep too much. I knew it! I'd told my mom I felt something was wrong. I would regularly run up to check if she was still breathing because she'd sleep for so long. I was panicked and petrified to find that the whites of her eyes were, indeed, yellow.

"Take her to the emergency room as soon as possible," the nurse said. "Tell them she is jaundiced."

My mother was unconvinced.

"She's stupid. The baby is fine. She can't even see her. You can't make these judgments over the phone."

"I still want to go."

"There's nothing to worry about! Just let her sleep! That's how they grow."

"I just want to go check. I want someone to see her." I kept insisting to my mother and to her father, until he finally relented and took us to the hospital.

They pricked the heel of her foot to get a drop of blood to check her bilirubin level. She didn't even flinch.

"She's such a good baby; she didn't even cry!"

"That's not a good thing," the nurse responded.

Her words stopped my heart cold. Of course it's not a good thing. How could she be so asleep that she doesn't even feel a prick strong enough to draw blood? A swift cloud of panic rose and enveloped me.

They immediately took her from me and put her under UV lights.

"Leave her under there," they said. "Don't hold her."

I sat and watched her as she lay naked in a clear plastic crib, and I cried. I was helpless. All I could do was stare at her and cry. I had never loved anyone in the world as much as I loved that tiny bundle, barely more than five pounds. I didn't even know it was possible to love that much. My arms and my body ached. All I wanted to do was hold her.

She eventually opened her eyes and began to wiggle. I instinctively reached in and held her in my arms and began to nurse her. I was so grateful that she was responsive!

"Put her back under the light!" the nurse bellowed. "Do you want her to get better or not? Holding her won't help. Put her down."

"But as soon as I put her down, she cries."

"So what? That's what babies do. I know it's hard on you, but it's not about you. You have to do what's right for her. She's going to take extra-long to recover if you keep doing that."

I had just won a battle over my mother because I insisted on listening to my own instincts regarding my daughter. I was a mother now, and I would have to start paying attention to my maternal instinct. I would not trust my mom or anyone else to tell me what was right for my daughter. My maternal instinct had already proven itself right when I insisted on bringing my daughter to emergency despite my mom's insistence that the baby was fine. My maternal instinct had been right before, so I was feeling confident that I should listen to it again. Despite the commands of Nurse Ratchet, I picked up my baby and cuddled her and nursed her whenever I could. The doctor came in and actually remarked about how quickly she had recovered. In your face, Nurse Ratchet! I knew it was because I had held her. Years later, I learned that research had shown that children recover from jaundice more quickly with skin-to-skin contact.

I was filled with a renewed focus on my baby. I would no longer just leave her in the crib or the swing so that I could cook his dinner or do my mother's laundry. I would put her needs first. They were demanding and mean, whereas she just sat there like an angel, so I'd prioritized them over her. But no more.

He would come home whenever he felt like it and comment on the messy house or look down his nose at me with my messy hair and spit-up on my shirt.

"Clean yourself up. You're disgusting. And why isn't this house clean?"

Frustrated, sleep-deprived, angry, and way beyond caring, I had a momentary lapse of judgment. In Arabic, as in French, nouns are gendered. When referring to the house, the question translated was: Why isn't *he* clean?

So, I answered, "Ask him."

As soon as the flippant words left my mouth, I regretted it. I braced myself, tensing up my whole body, unsure of where the blow would land.

"I'm asking you!" he bellowed.

Stunned by the absurdity of his response—that he was talking to me, not the house, I burst out laughing. I guess taking care of a baby all on your own with no Internet to guide you, with no friends to call, with no outlet—it all caught up with me. I let out a hearty roar, and he knocked the wind out of me in response.

It was one of the worst beatings he ever gave me. His ego couldn't handle that I was laughing at him. I was a mere woman laughing at *him*. So he proceeded to show me who was boss. I was so exhausted from taking care of his child that I barely reacted. How much more could he possibly hurt me? I was already depleted.

I was married, but I was essentially a single mother. He never showed the slightest interest in our daughter. But then one day, he did.

As I kissed her little fingers that were wrapped tightly around my finger, he leaned in and asked:

"Is she cleaned?"

"Yes, I just gave her a bath," I said.

"No, I mean, is she fixed?"

"I don't understand what you mean."

"No, no," my mother interjected. "We do that later. When she's older."

Then I understood. He was talking about female genital mutilation. He wanted to take a razor blade and mutilate my little miracle. A defensive anger I didn't know I still had rose up in me like lava. I never had the courage to fight for myself, but I would have jumped out the window with my baby to get her away from him. However, my mother's response was buying me some time.

"Are you sure? We better do it right away. I will not have my daughter be unclean."

"Yes, yes," my mother said. "We'll take her to Egypt and have it done as soon as we can."

I was filled with a sense of urgency. I knew I would fight for my daughter. I decided I would get her out of this house before they had the chance to hurt her. I would make sure that she was free from both of them before she was even old enough to retain memories of who they were.

The only other time he had anything to say to my daughter, it was something equally heinous. He'd recite a rhyme to her whenever he saw me changing her.

"Wear new clothes. Live with gratitude. Die a martyr."

First of all, what does wearing new clothes have to do with dying a martyr? Second of all, don't talk about my daughter dying! I was completely enraged, scared, upset, and saddened by those stupid words. I did everything I could to avoid changing her in front of him. I have since seen videos of men sending their little children, like Trojan horses, to die as martyrs in suicide bombings. That is the power of brainwashing. It overrides your natural, instinctual, human reactions of love and empathy. It demands that you suppress these instincts. It demands that you act in an immoral and corrupt way toward your children because that is what Allah wants. You have to overcome your most basic instinct to protect your child in order to meet the demands of the religion—like the story of Abraham and his willingness to slaughter his son for God. That is not virtue. That is madness. But that action was so revered that it spawned three world religions. What kind of bloodthirsty, maniacal god would make such a demand of its creation? It's like a scene out of the most horrific of horror movies, too terrifying to even imagine. Yet this was the pinnacle of virtue: to be willing to sacrifice your child for God.

I named my baby after my mother. It was my last-ditch attempt at winning her love. I was at peak desperation when I did that. I had tried everything to win her over. This had to do the trick. I regretted it immediately. But I placated myself with the justification that my mom would be nicer to her if she was her namesake, and I was right. Such was my mother's ego that she unabashedly gave preference to my daughter in the way that she used to give preference to my sister. What a cruel fate. Rather than rejoice at the karma of seeing my sister's daughters being demoted to second-class-granddaughters, though, I was disgusted. I didn't want my daughter to get a sense of superiority over her cousins, and my heart broke for those little girls, as I knew exactly how they felt. Intimately.

I was used to being stuck between wanting my mother's love and wanting to be as far away from her as possible, but these days I was leaning more toward wanting to be away from her. When I held my baby girl in my arms and felt this foreign surge of love flow through me, I finally saw everything from a different perspective. I suddenly could not imagine how my mom could have been so cruel to me for all these years. I would not hesitate to protect my daughter without regard even for my own life! How could she have done all those things to me?

How could she have stood idly by as I was tortured by the men she brought into my life? How could she have not protected me?

I concluded that she couldn't possibly have felt the same way about me as I felt about my daughter. I wasn't sure why. I wasn't sure if it was because of me or because of her. Then again, how could it be because of me? I was a newborn! I couldn't take the blame when I was just a newborn. That blame was placed on me later, and I internalized it. But I could see now that it was all false—she must not have *ever* felt this way about me. You can't feel this way and then just lose it after a few years. This was life-changing, soul-altering, deep, and unconditional love. I didn't cause her to hate me because I was so wretched, as she had me believe. I had never had a chance. She never loved me to begin with.

AL QAEDA

I was still stuck in a house with my mother and the beast she had forced me to marry. I couldn't figure out which one of them was worse, as they seemed to take turns. The only time things were bearable was when they were on the outs for one reason or another. As long as they were both tight, I was toast. I would be the punchline of their jokes.

And the two of them were uncharacteristically tight. I chalked it up to the fact that they both spoke the same language. I didn't really care to spend time with either one of them, anyway. Let them hang out together and stay the hell out of my way. I was happy hanging out with my baby. So when he pulled me aside one night and told me that he wanted us to move out with our new baby, I was really surprised.

"Your mom is not a good person."

Well, yeah. I knew that, but how did he know that?

"What are you talking about? The two of you are like peas in a pod."

"And it's wrong. We shouldn't be. You and I should be that close. You are my wife. Not her."

We did have a weird thing going on, there's no doubt. My mom, at the age of fifty-something, had decided to start wearing a niqab. She was very clearly trying to appease him. The two of them seemed more like the married couple, and I was the cook, cleaner, and nanny.

Normally, people would say how lucky I was to have my mom with me when I have a new baby. You'd think so, but no. My mother was just an added burden. She was just as demanding as he was. I was going so flat-out serving the both of them, my daughter was always expected to be third in line.

As long as the two of them were in this unholy alliance, I was trapped. I decided to accept his offer to move out, as it would serve to divide them. My thought was that if I could at least separate them, I'd only have to deal with one of them at a time, and I knew my mom would be much easier to wriggle away from than he would be. I figured that once I got them separated, I would somehow make my way over to her side.

I told my mom that he wanted to move away from her. I figured she'd be upset, insulted, or hurt, but I wasn't prepared for the explosiveness of her reaction. She completely flew off the handle in a way that was impressive, even for someone like her who loses her mental balance quite regularly.

When he came home, she rained terror on him. I was expecting him to get mad at me for telling her, but he didn't. He was glad she knew. He was glad he wasn't the one who had to tell her.

"I am going to sleep at Amr's house tonight," he said to me. "You pack up everything that is ours. I already have a place. We can leave tomorrow."

Tomorrow? Something serious was going on between them.

He left again, and my mother continued to pace and swear and yell even though he wasn't there to hear it. And then she started to cough. Her coughing got more and more violent. I ran down to the kitchen to get her a glass of water. When I returned, she was bent over the bathroom sink coughing up blood. Simultaneously, blood was pouring from her nose. I stared at her with the glass of water in my hand, unable to move. She finally managed to coherently gurgle between coughs.

"911!"

I was in a frenzy. I had never seen that much blood in my life. I ran downstairs to the phone and then back up to her again, then back down again and up again, I don't know how many times I did that before I finally stopped and picked up the phone to dial 911.

When the ambulance arrived to pick her up, I hesitated. I had never left the house without him before. Was I allowed to go with her? Would I get in trouble? I surmised that this was an emergency, and hopefully he would understand. I realized that there was a high chance that he wouldn't, but I took the risk anyway. My baby and I rode with them in the ambulance. When we arrived at the hospital, my mother was rushed off, and my daughter and I were left to sit in the waiting room.

We weren't there very long before I was approached by a man and a woman.

"Are you Yasmine?" the woman asked me gently, almost whispering.

"Yes." I assumed they had news about my mom. I started to ask them what would make her suddenly start to bleed like that.

"No," she said. "We're from CSIS."

"Did they move her from emergency?" I asked. I assumed CSIS was the name of a ward in the hospital.

"No, CSIS stands for Canadian Security Intelligence Service."

"I don't know what you mean. What's going on?"

"It's like the CIA," the man responded. "Like the Canadian CIA."

"Oh, I didn't know we had one." I still didn't understand why they had ambushed me in the hospital. "Did I do something wrong? Why are you here?"

"No, you're fine. We have been wanting to speak to you for a long time, but we could never get you alone. We're actually really glad to finally get an opportunity to speak with you."

"About what?"

"Is your husband coming to the hospital?"

My husband? What did he have to do with anything?

"No, he's sleeping over at a friend's house."

This was long before cell phones were commonplace. I had left him a note in the house, just in case he got back before we did. I didn't have his friend's number.

"So he doesn't know you're here?"

"No. I mean, unless he goes home and reads the note."

They talked quietly together while I stared at my baby sleeping in her car seat, wondering if my mom would live or die.

"Okay, you and I are going to go to a private room to talk, and my partner will stay here. If your husband comes back, he'll come to tell us, okay?"

"Okay." I had no idea what was going on, but I was not about to question a CSIS officer.

She ushered me and my sleeping baby into a room. She explained to me that I was married to an Al Qaeda member. I had no idea what that meant. This was pre-9/11, and the Western world was generally unaware of that group. She asked me all sorts of questions. Most I couldn't answer. Then she asked me if I had ever heard the name Osama bin Laden. My eyes quickly darted up to hers.

"Has he mentioned that name?"

"Well, he found a magazine with Osama bin Laden's picture in it, and he got really worked up. He asked me why I had it. He asked me if I knew who the guy was. And then he told me to get rid of it as quickly as possible. I couldn't figure out why he was overreacting. It seemed like he was accusing me of something."

I had no idea why this woman from CSIS was also asking me about bin Laden.

"Okay, try to remember if there's anything else that we haven't talked about that might be important."

"I don't know what's important. I don't know what we're talking about."

"Anything at all. Any other friends that you haven't mentioned. Anything you might have overheard?"

"I don't think so. He hardly ever brings people to the house. He always goes out. He's always at his friend Amr's house. Sometimes for days." They weren't interested in Amr at all.

"Where does he get his money from? He just started a company. What's that all about?"

"I have no idea. He was unemployed when I married him. I faxed resumes randomly to everyone, and he eventually got a call back from a seafood warehouse. He's been working there for a few months. I don't actually know anything about the company. I just know it's called 4U Enterprises."

"Does he have any skills that you know of? What's the purpose of the business?"

"I don't know. He's not very educated."

"How do you know?"

"Well, I knew his English wasn't that great, but I saw him write his name in Arabic once, and it was like a child wrote it. I mean, my Arabic reading and writing is even better than his."

I had no clue what he could possibly start a business about. And I had no idea where he got his money. His job paid minimum wage, but somehow he always had money. He did frequently bellow "911" over the phone with his friends and then laugh. I thought it was strange enough to ask him about it, but he raised his finger, as he often would, and flicked it toward the door. "Out!" That's how he would dismiss me, like the way you'd shoo a bug.

I didn't tell her about the weird 9/11 incident because it wasn't significant at the time. In hindsight it was very significant, but I doubt they would have made the connection, anyway.

When it was clear that I had nothing more to offer, she shared with me that the man I married had entered Canada as a refugee from Afghanistan with a fake Saudi Arabian passport because his Egyptian passport was flagged. It was flagged because he was deemed a terrorist by Egyptian authorities. Egypt had a warrant out for his arrest. But CSIS didn't want to arrest him; they wanted to learn about his plan and purpose for coming to Canada.

I remembered him telling me stories about his dad being held and questioned by the Egyptian police. He told me that's why he couldn't go back. I asked him why the Egyptian police was after him, and he said it was because Mubarak was a criminal and a dictator, and the whole government was corrupt. He never mentioned that he did anything to deserve attention from the authorities.

But again, this was not a red flag. In Egypt, if you insulted Mubarak in your own home and a neighbour overheard you, you could be arrested the next day. So, it was no surprise to me that the police department was corrupt. The whole country was corrupt.

I should have been more scared and horrified of him than I was, but I had no idea of the true potential of Al Qaeda or their ilk. Jihadi wannabes were common in Muslim countries. They're always bumbling around, yelling "death to America" and complaining that no one is religious enough. I saw them all over Egypt. You recognize them by their unkempt beards (but no moustache) and pants that are an inch above their ankles-they dressed as the Prophet Mohammed dressed. No one takes them seriously. They are usually uneducated and ostracized by the rest of society. They have a lot of anger because they feel they are the righteous, and it's frustrating for them that they are not being recognized for their greatness. People humour them instead. They also tread carefully around them, as they are known to be volatile. And if I'm being honest, there's also a quiet reverence at these men taking their religion so seriously—it makes other Muslims feel ashamed that they are not as devout. Their quest is to give their life for Allah in a suicide bombing or something. Most of them are concentrated in Palestine, part of Hamas. They flock to areas where Muslims are in conflict with others and look for an opportunity to become a *shaheed*, martyr for Allah. But none of that was of any concern in Canada. They had no power here.

Later I had asked him why he had gone to Afghanistan in the first place. He said that when he was young, they lived in a poorer part of Egypt. Then when he was a teenager, his father (an engineer) got a really good job, and they moved up to a higher class neighbourhood. In Egypt, the distinctions between classes is vast. The differences are not only geographic, but also in the language, mannerisms, and clothing choices—everything is starkly different. Essam had trouble fitting in with the rich boys who made fun of him for his low-class roots. An outcast among his peers, he was approached by jihadis—a common story of how people are recruited into gangs. They promised him that he was destined for greater things than his bullies. He was destined for parts of Heaven that only the martyrs who die in the name of Allah are privy to. They embraced him and fulfilled him with their simple message of purpose. He was part of a tight-knit boys club. He had all the camaraderie that was out of his reach in that elitist school. He belonged.

My mom insisted that he was never involved in terrorist activities, that he only "trained little boys on how to use guns to protect themselves from the Russians." I asked him if that was true. I asked him if he was ever involved beyond that, and he never gave me a straight answer. Strangely, he seemed uncomfortable responding. Somehow, with the questions coming from me, he felt his responses were shameful. I can imagine he would brag loudly with others about his involvements, but with me he made general, sheepish statements like "I had to do what I had to do to protect my brothers" and "killing for Allah is not wrong, it is the greatest honour."

Still, I half-heartedly questioned him or tried to listen for anything that might be helpful so that I could relay it to CSIS. But my main focus was to get away from him soon. He and my mom were definitely over.

She had apparently driven her blood pressure up so high because she was so angry at him, that's why she had bled spontaneously from her nose and mouth. She wanted nothing more to do with him.

This was good news for me, because now she might actually help me get away from him. I just needed to wait for the right moment. I wanted my mom to be established in her new apartment, so my baby and I could go join her. I hesitated because I was scared. I was waiting for the circumstances to be easier, so that I would be less scared.

ESCAPE

As I was waiting for the right time to escape, I found out I was pregnant again. I was home alone with just my nine-month-old baby when I took the test. I was told by him and my mom that I couldn't get pregnant if I was nursing. Obviously, they were both wrong. I think now how differently my life would have unfolded if I'd had access to something like the Internet back then. I screamed and wailed and yelled and cursed for two hours until my throat was raw and my tears had run dry. I was exhausted. I was prepared to be a single mother to one baby girl, but not to two. How would I live with two? How would I support two? My fate was sealed. This child was my death sentence. My life was over. I should have left. Why did I wait? I could have been free, but now this was it. I had to submit fully. There was no escape. This was my life. As it had been my mother's life, and the life of countless other Muslim women.

I lived with this dread and anger and sadness for weeks. In that time, of course, I was beaten up just as regularly as I always had been. At one point, he was kicking my back as I lay in the fetal position on the floor. I tried to tell him that he was going to hurt the baby, but he didn't care. I just lay there too depressed to care either. I used my old trick of going into myself and blocking out the pain. I just waited for him to tire himself. My back and backside were so bruised, I couldn't sit down comfortably for days.

To calm my fears that he had hurt the baby, I took another pregnancy test, and it was still positive, so I thought everything would be okay. I didn't understand that pregnancy tests just detect if a hormone is present; they don't determine if the baby is alive. At my ultrasound, the technician paused in the middle of the procedure and left the room.

"What's happening?" I asked when she returned.

"You'll need to go see your doctor immediately."

"Why won't you tell me?"

"I can't tell you, but your doctor is waiting for you. Please meet her at this clinic—now." She passed me an address on a small sheet of paper and ushered me out the door.

When my ex and I arrived at the clinic, my doctor told me that I had had a missed miscarriage and that I would have to go in for a D and C immediately. A missed miscarriage meant that my baby did not have a heartbeat. I was carrying a dead baby. I had killed my baby. I was so unhappy about the pregnancy that I had killed the baby. My tears and turmoil and anguish had killed him. He knew he was unwanted. I did this. It never once occurred to me that my husband's violent beating could have been the cause; I took all the blame on entirely.

I barely had time to deal with the fact that I had murdered my child before I was put under general anesthetic. They removed my baby—which I had killed—and I was free to go home.

Although the guilt of what I had done weighed heavily on me for years afterward, in that moment, I knew I would not squander my opportunity to escape again. I would not wait for the perfect time to leave. I would leave now. I had gotten a glimpse of what my life would be like if I hesitated. So, I was determined not to make the same mistake. I would make a clean break to save my baby who was still alive. I told him I wanted to go to my mom's house for about a week to recover from the procedure. He was hesitant, but he eventually took me, as he was nervous that he might be expected to help with his daughter.

When he dropped me off, I knew I would never go back. There was nothing there that I needed. I had my daughter, and that was all that mattered.

The next morning, after my mom left for work, I immediately searched through the Yellow Pages and called Lawyer Referral to get information for a lawyer who would be willing to help me get a divorce, a restraining order, and full custody ASAP. I was lucky to find a lawyer nearby. I covered myself—every inch of skin, even my eyes—in my black shroud. I pulled on the thick gloves and socks that had been delivered from Saudi Arabia, and I walked out the door. As I hopped on the city bus with my daughter, I panicked for a moment that I wouldn't make it home before my mom came home from teaching Islamic studies at the Islamic school.

I found the building easily. My heart was beating really fast as I walked through the glass doors and into the elevator, awkwardly carrying my baby in her car seat. I was grateful she was sleeping. I needed to be fast—there was no time for distractions. As I walked into the lawyer's office, I saw two women chatting with each other. They suddenly turned to me, shock in their eyes. One stood where she was, just staring at me. The other walked over and greeted me as if she were expecting me. She was the lawyer.

"Come in. Sit down. Are you okay? Can I get you some water?"

I wondered why she was making a fuss. I'm sure I wasn't the first woman who had called asking to make an appointment for full custody, a divorce, and a restraining order. It never dawned on me then that the sight of a figure completely shrouded in black entering their office was not an everyday occurrence!

The lawyer continued to speak to me in a confident, authoritative manner. I got the immediate sense that she was a no-nonsense kind of person and had everything under control. She did everything pro bono as quickly as the law would allow her. She was so slick and awesome that I wanted to be her. I reconnected with her years later. I brought my new husband and my new daughter for her to see. I wanted her to know that she had helped make my life possible. She still had that no-nonsense manner. *I was just doing my job*, her attitude conveyed. But it was so much more than that. She saved my life. She made my life possible. She knew it would be difficult for me to get to her again, so she prepared all the papers immediately and had me sign everything before I left.

"Is there a phone I can reach you at? If there's anything else?"

"No. You can't call me. I'll call you."

"Ok, call me tomorrow. Everything is going to be fine."

I was so grateful. So happy. And so scared.

I had been talking to him over the phone like I normally did as I waited for him to get served. I didn't want him to have any idea what was going on until it was all over. When I was finally sure it was all done and that he was going to be served with the divorce papers the next day, I told him.

He was absolutely blindsided. He hadn't seen it coming at all. I actually felt bad that I'd pulled the rug out from under him like that. But he got me back just as good when he told me that my mother had been pressuring him to have sex with her pretty much the whole time we were married. He said that he tried to get her to agree to leave him alone, but she wouldn't. He said that's why he decided to move away from her. I told him I didn't believe his lies. I told him it was a pretty disgusting story to make up to get back at me. But I'm pretty sure every word of it was true.

He reminded me of the times he tried to get me to see it for myself. And though I remembered the incidents he was referring to, I never would have put two and two together. It was just too far outside the realm of possibility.

"When does Essam usually want you?" my mother had asked me one day.

"What do you mean? I don't know. Whenever he wants."

"No, but try to think. Is it a specific time of day? Is it when you are wearing something particular?"

"Why are you asking? I don't know! I guess whenever I'm in my bathrobe around him. That's why I don't like to shower when he's home."

"Oh. Ok."

A few weeks later, he asked me to go into his office.

"What's going on? You never let me in here."

"Just wait."

"What am I waiting for?"

"You'll see."

And that's when my mom walked in with nothing on but a towel. Wet from her shower. In her hand, she was carrying a black-and-white photo of herself when she was about thirty years younger.

"What is she doing here?" she said to Essam, her eyes darting at me.

"What are you doing here?" he asked her back.

"I—I brought you this picture." He didn't reach his hand out to take it. Instead, he looked over at me and gestured for me to take it. I took it out of her hand.

"I have no idea what's happening here. Why are you coming in here in a towel bringing him a picture? This is so weird," I said.

"Why did you bring that picture to me?" Essam asked.

"If you don't want it, I'll keep it!" she said. She ripped the photo from hand and turned on her heel and defiantly walked out.

Essam looked at me expectantly.

"What?"

"You don't see?"

"I see," I said, "but I don't understand. I have to go. The baby is up."

Looking back now, I can't believe how stupid and naive I was. He had tried multiple times. And each time I was equally clueless.

Before hanging up, he told me he didn't care what I did with my silly Canadian laws, because Islamically, I was still his wife. When I died, if I made it to Heaven, I would still be his wife. And if I didn't make it, he would. He would be a martyr, and he would request me, and I would be his wife for eternity. There was no escape. I would still be married to him, because only a man can divorce his wife, not vice versa. In the eyes of Allah, I would still be married to him, unless *he* made the decision for the marriage to be over.

So I asked him to divorce me. The way this is done is the husband simply utters the words *you are divorced* in Arabic three times, and, poof, the marriage is over. He refused to say it. He said he was coming to get me.

Of course when he arrived, I would not buzz him in. I ignored the phone. I turned off all the lights and pretended I wasn't home. He stood at the entrance to the building and screamed in Arabic.

"Give me back my wife! I want my wife! You just wait till I get you! I will cut your face! You think you can leave me? No man will ever want you when I am finished with you! You are mine, do you hear me? You are mine or you are dead."

I sat in the dark, rocking my baby in my arms, waiting for him to leave or for the cops to arrive, whichever came first. I was absolutely petrified that someone would be going in or out of the building and that they would let him in.

HOUSE ARREST

I lived in constant fear for the next year as I waited for the divorce to be finalized. Since he refused to sign the divorce papers, I would have to wait a year before the divorce could go through with only my signature. Not that a legal divorce gave me much freedom anyway. As he had told me many times, I would only escape temporarily, because he would tear me apart in Heaven.

Since I was not divorced Islamically, in the eyes of Allah, I was still his wife. In Heaven, men are given the choice to be with whichever of their Earth wives they choose to be with. Since a man is allowed to have up to four wives (at a time), it is quite plausible that he would have had plenty over his lifetime. He may not want all of them to be with him in

Heaven, so he gets to choose his favourites to join him. In Heaven, he's not limited to four, he can have all the wives he wants.

These wives are, of course, in addition to the *hur*, the nonhuman virgin sex slaves. They have skin so white you can see their veins, big round breasts, and they do not urinate or defecate, let alone get their period. They do not have any will other than to do what they are told. Basically, Mohammed invented realistic sex dolls way before the Japanese did.

Women do not get a say in this. If a man chooses his wife in Heaven, then that is where she will spend eternity. Islam, as you might have realized, is an extremely gendered religion. Women are only mentioned in relation to men. To illustrate, a dog is not communicated to directly by a trainer. The trainer speaks to the owner and informs them how to treat the dog. This is the relationship between Allah (the trainer) and women (the dogs).

Because of this, there are no revelations to describe who a woman gets to be with in Heaven. It is not even mentioned. No one asks a sex slave in a slave market if she wants to be with her owner. That would be ridiculous.

I could hope and infer that if Heaven is supposed to be everything I want, I would not have to be with him; but this would directly contradict the revelation that *he* is the one who gets to choose if he wants to be with me.

This stuff haunted me. I felt like I'd have a few years of reprieve on Earth, but then I might end up stuck with him for eternity anyway.

I never left the apartment at all for fear that he might be lurking around a corner. He had described to me in intimate detail what he would do to me if I ever tried to leave him. And I believed every word of it. He promised to cut my face so I would be so ugly that no man would ever want to look at me, let alone touch me. That was his biggest concern. I was his—the thought of another man touching his property enraged him.

I lived in this state of fear for a long time but was finally able to relax when CSIS contacted me to ask me to verify him in a photo. The photo was indeed of him. He was behind bars in Egypt. His eyes were full of murderous rage, and his body language was terrifying. He was literally like a caged rabid animal. Cognitively, I knew I was holding a black-and-white newspaper clipping, but my heart beat with an intense fear, as if he were right in front of me. That image is burned into my mind forever—the image of a monumental rage and aggression being held back by bars. It was all but inconceivable to me that someone had managed to cage a tornado. He looked like he would rip the bars out of the wall at any second. I can't imagine what he did with all that energy, with no way to release it. Usually, I had been the one to fulfill that role for him.

Being held in Mubarak's prison was his greatest fear. He wanted to die a martyr, not be held by a government he despised. This was the most humiliating predicament he could ever possibly find himself in. I actually felt sorry for him. But I was so relieved at the same time.

As terrifying as it was, it was strange to think that I could finally begin thinking about starting my life over again. On our last visit together, the CSIS officer gifted me with a beautiful leather bag. She said it was for me to use when I finished my education and became a teacher. She exhibited the knock-me-off-my-feet kindness I'd come to expect from nonbelievers. She congratulated me on my freedom.

I guess I was free, but I didn't feel free. I still moved cautiously and carefully. What if he escaped? What if he had a friend around ready to enact his revenge? Where was his friend Amr?

I learned then that Amr had disappeared at the same time. Was he in an Egyptian prison, too? No. He wasn't. There were reports that he had died at almost exactly the same time that Essam was imprisoned. I presumed that Amr was likely working for the FBI. That's why CSIS didn't show any interest in anything I had to say about him. I had lived in that area my whole life and I knew all the Muslims, but this Amr guy just happened to appear out of nowhere at the exact same time as Essam, and then disappear on the exact same timeline as well. It was too much of a coincidence. Most notably, when I saw Amr briefly, he never struck me as evil. He didn't have those sinister and judgmental eyes that are typical of jihadi types.

Even though he was gone, and his friend was gone, it was not as easy as flipping a switch. For years I had been in an abusive relationship that had annihilated whomever I once was. I felt an irrational sense of guilt that he was in prison. I worried about what he was eating—he was such a picky eater. I can see now that I had been deeply enveloped in Stockholm syndrome.

On top of all the internal struggles, I had to manage being a mother. For the next few months, I lived with my mother, took an online course from the local college, and tried to piece my life back together. I took courses online to be home with my daughter and also because I was still afraid of going out in public.

If you are caged long enough, freedom feels weird, unfamiliar, and uncomfortable. Even though I hardly left home, when I did, I still wore a niqab. There was no defining moment when I ripped it off my face and began to breathe free air. It was a slow, gruelling process filled with self-doubt, sadness, and copious amounts of fear. Once again I would try to heal from having the rug pulled out from under me, from the debilitating fear of being psychologically slapped down. Once again, I would try to stand up on my own two feet. But I was much more broken this time, and much more tired. And I had the weight of a child in my arms.

My brother had just moved in as well. He had lost his job because he was constantly late for work. He lived in an apartment that was directly above his work downtown. He quite literally just had to take the elevator down, but he was always late. So they fired him. He fled from his apartment in the middle of the night to avoid having to pay that month's rent. Yet he had the gall to be judgmental toward me.

"What are you going to do with your life now?"

"Live."

"What is that supposed to mean? How are you going to live?"

One morning he was sharing a bowl of grapes with my little girl who was just a toddler at the time.

"Why won't she let me put it in her mouth?" He sounded irritated.

"She likes to feed herself," I said. "I taught her to bite the grapes, so she doesn't choke on them."

"What's the big deal? She can put a whole grape in her mouth!" he said derisively.

"It's a choking hazard; she's just a baby. It's better for her to bite it."

"I don't see why she can't just pop it in her mouth."

"Why does this concern you?" Now I was getting irritated.

"I want to feed her!"

"Well, she wants to feed herself. Just leave her alone."

"She needs to learn to listen. I said, put in in your mouth!" He was yelling, and as he did, he grabbed my child, flipped her horizontally and savagely shoved a handful of grapes into her screaming mouth.

I leaped up and threw myself between him and my daughter. In response, he punched and kicked me. I ignored him as much as I could and focused all my energy and attention on confirming that she had spit out all the grapes and that she would be okay. Once I saw that her mouth was empty and that she would not choke, I exhaled, exhausted and relieved.

He pummelled my face with one hand as he held me captive by the hair with his other to keep me from running. I went to my familiar spot. I retreated inside myself and went limp. It had been a while. I'd rarely gone limp during my marriage. Essam's abuse was usually more concentrated and short—one strong punch to the face. But this beating by my brother was more reminiscent of my childhood—successive flailing until all his frustration was released.

Would I never escape this life? I grew up in a home where I was abused, I married a man who abused me, and I escaped that to a home where my brother abused me. How would I get myself out of this cycle before my daughter slipped into this downward spiral as well? Between punches, I saw glimpses of her, not even two years old, watching her mother get the shit beaten out of her, and it wasn't phasing her in the least. She wasn't even slightly bothered by the scene in front of her. It was as commonplace for her as it had been for me.

This had to stop. I had to end this cycle. I would not allow her to be on the receiving end of this one day because of my inability to protect her from that life.

My unresponsive body seemed to shake my brother out of whatever diabolical temper tantrum he had been in. He suddenly shook me to check if I was still alive.

"I thought I had killed you!" he exhaled in a loud whisper.

"Get off me."

"Are you okay? Why weren't you moving!"

That was the last time my brother hit me. I barely saw him after that. He talked to me about it, so I know it scared him, and I know he carried that fear with him for years. But it didn't scare him enough to prevent him from beating up other women who entered his life after that. He was imprisoned on domestic abuse charges multiple times and he has struggled with substance abuse and mental health issues. He even had bouts of homelessness.

My brother suffered more than I did growing up. He was definitely beat up more than I was, and he constantly had his "manhood" challenged by my mother and the monster she married. In their eyes, a "real man" needs to be overly aggressive and the stereotypical macho-type. My brother did not fit that bill. He preferred nature shows and video games—he was not interested in sports or wrestling or any of the typical machismo pastimes. He took a lot of abuse, and he showed signs of cracking in his late teens. My mom ignored the drugs prescribed by our family doctor and preferred to pray away all his depression, OCD, etc. Obviously, her prayers did nothing, and my brother just continued to spiral. In the short time we spent together recently, he would get angry because he "heard" my husband and me talking negatively about him behind his back. He admitted that he couldn't discern between real life and his mind playing tricks on him when it came to hearing these voices, but he had trouble believing me when I told him it wasn't real. Things went downhill very quickly as his rage escalated, and we eventually severed ties. He is what I could have become if I hadn't gotten myself out of that world.

On the day that I received my last beating from a man, my brother, I realized I had literally no one on this planet I could rely on. Was Allah up there looking out for me? That didn't seem very plausible, but I was in no position to start considering that I didn't even have supernatural support, either. That's the only semblance of hope that I had. As far as I knew, no one on this planet was here to help me, but maybe Allah would. I needed to sort out my life.

I could not continue to live with my mother and my brother. I knew I had to get my daughter out of this treacherous house full of cruelty and abuse. She was all I had in this world, and I was all she had. I was responsible for her, but I couldn't look to her for support—my role was to support her. I had to get her out of danger. I wish I had gotten her out sooner. That traumatic day cannot be erased from her mind. To this day, my daughter still has anxiety about choking while eating. For every meal of her entire life, she needs to have water next to her, as she gets panicked that she might choke. For every meal of her entire life, I have to feel gut-wrenching pangs of guilt and regret that I did not get her out of harm's way soon enough. And now she carries the internal scars forever. Because of me.

ON OUR OWN

My mother was absolutely against the idea of me moving out; she couldn't fathom how I could even suggest it. Respectable Muslim women do not live on their own. They go from their father's house to their husband's house. The thought of her daughter living on her own was inconceivable to my mom. But I couldn't stay there.

I knew that moving out would upset her, but I was finally willing to openly defy her for the sake of my daughter. I never had the strength to stand up to her for myself, but when it came to protecting my daughter, I found the strength.

I applied for social assistance, and I spoke with the manager of my mother's building. I figured that her resistance would be less if I were in the same building as she was. He told me that he had a one-bedroom that he could rent out to me, but it was on a different floor. I thought about waiting until an apartment on her floor opened up, but I decided against it. In the same building should be close enough for her to keep an eye on me. It's not like I was a virgin anymore! After marriage, a Muslim woman is not nearly as fiercely controlled by her family. I moved as soon as I could. I knew she wouldn't be happy about it, but I figured she'd be okay with me being in the same building.

But my mother was livid that I had moved out. I might as well have rented a place across town. She spat out every insult that was a synonym for *whore* that she could muster. Despite it all, I still moved out.

On my first day in my new apartment, I filled out applications to the universities that were nearby. I was accepted into my first choice. My mother was also livid that I was applying to university. She kept trying to get me to meet other suitors, other potential husbands, but I was not going to fall down the same hole a second time.

Slowly, over the next few months as I waited for classes to start, I started to heal. I remember taking off my niqab for the first time and feeling like my face was naked. I felt as vulnerable and self-conscious as if I were topless. I thought everyone would stare at my bare face, but no one cared. My little toddler was the only one who found it strange that my face was bare. She would try to lift up the cloth of the hijab to cover my face again. Bit by bit I started to wear long skirts instead of the *abaya*. And I slowly started to rediscover who I had been before my marriage.

Because I still felt I needed to appease my mom by getting an apartment that was in the same building as hers, the rent was much higher than I could afford. And since my mother wouldn't let me move out into an apartment I could afford, occasionally I would ask her for money for rent or food.

"No," she'd respond. "Aren't you Miss Independent Woman? If you want to do it all on your own, then go! Do it on your own!"

"Can I just borrow some money to get some groceries then? I don't even have milk. I only have enough money exactly for the rent."

"You don't have to pay rent! You can come back and live with me. I am not wasting my money."

"Okay, but can I borrow some money for now?"

"I said *no*!"

"Are you going to let your granddaughter starve?" I reached into her purse and took her credit card.

"If you try to use that, I will call the bank and tell them it was stolen."

"No you won't. You know I need to buy her food. She's your granddaughter!"

"I don't care! You made these stupid decisions; you can live with them. And if you try to take my car, I will call the police and tell them it was stolen, too!"

I called her bluff. I took my baby, my mother's car keys, and her credit card, and I went grocery shopping anyway. As I shopped, I gave my mom an ultimatum in my head. If she does call the bank or the police, that will be the last straw. Even for my mom, it seemed like that would just be too much.

I find it strange that I even doubted that she would. As I went to pay for the groceries, the cashier informed me that the card was stolen. He knew me as I frequented that grocery shop a lot.

"I am supposed to call the police," he said sheepishly as his eyes darted between me and my daughter. "But it's okay. I won't. But I can't ring these groceries through."

"It's okay, thank you." I felt like someone had punched me in the throat. Once again, a supposed filthy, dirty nonbeliever was kinder to me than my own family.

When I got back to the car, all I could think of was that she likely called the police about the stolen car, too. And now my daughter and I might get arrested. I had to get back home as soon as possible.

That was the day I realized that there was literally *nothing* that was beneath my mother. I had an open can of evaporated milk that I had taken from the Mosque kitchen. It's not really stealing, I told myself. It's there for people to use. So what if I happen to be using it at home instead of in the Mosque? I mixed it with water and fed it to my child. That was her dinner. She was two years old now, and a bottle of milk was not a sufficient meal. I wished I hadn't stopped nursing her—at least that was free food—but I had to stop when I found out that I was pregnant with her sibling. I rolled over and cried myself to sleep.

THE ELEPHANT

Once I started university, things became even more difficult. I needed money for books and supplies, transportation, childcare—I couldn't do it anymore. I was forced to go back to living with my mom and my brother. The four of us moved into a town house in a neighbouring city. I had to take four buses to get to university and four buses to get home again.

If I got four hours of sleep, I would consider it a good night. I was taking five courses per semester, as I wanted to finish my undergrad degree as soon as possible so I could get my degree in Education. Then I could become a teacher and finally begin to make some money. I was racking up student loans, so most of my money would have to go to pay all that off eventually. But I couldn't think about that now. I just had to get through day by day.

Everything in my life was difficult but bearable except for the constant nagging and pressure from my mother. She was driving me crazy. I would try to minimize our fights, but sometimes I just had to react.

"I bought you a new shirt!" my mother exclaimed.

My daughter went running over to see what was in the bag. My mom pulled out a dark-green T-shirt. My daughter squirmed away when my mom tried to put it on her.

"What's wrong with you?"

"I let her choose her own clothes," I intervened. "She doesn't like green. She only likes pink or purple."

"Are you stupid?" my mom said to my daughter. "Green is a beautiful colour."

"She's not stupid!" I yelled. "People can like different things. That doesn't make them stupid. She doesn't want it. Stop forcing her to like what you like!"

It ended up being a huge fight, where I was the ungrateful daughter for not graciously accepting a gift. The fact that she was physically putting something on my child's body that she did not want to wear was not a relevant point. I might have reacted strongly, but I knew what it was like to have someone force clothes on you that you don't want to wear, and I was *not* going to let my daughter know what that felt like.

As well, the fact that my daughter was being considered stupid for not liking the same things my mom liked induced Hades-level rage in me. That was my whole life right there. Trying to control me so much so that I didn't even know if I had my own opinions! I would not let my daughter experience that. She will choose her clothes, and she will have her own opinions. And if she only wants to wear pink or purple, then she'll only wear pink or purple.

Because I was attending university now, my self-confidence was growing. It was emboldening me to defy my mother more. I was a few years older than most of my classmates, and I had significantly more life experience. This was especially helpful in a child psychology course I was taking. As the professor and I were the only parents in the class, quite often I would be the one student in the room who could easily understand what the professor was talking about. Class discussions were commonly the professor and me trying to explain things to my younger classmates. Now my voice was relevant. My opinions and experiences had merit. I wasn't the stupid, useless dimwit that I was taken for at home.

In fact, I could even start to see errors in my mother's judgments. But could I be so brazen as to think that I could possibly be smarter than she was? That seemed way outside the realm of possibility, but I decided to test my suspicion.

My mother had wanted to buy a Volvo. For whatever reason, she was hell-bent on the idea. Her first step was to approach Muslim used car salespeople because, of course, only Muslims could be trusted. To me, that idea was completely ridiculous.

"Which god you pray to is no indication of your ability to be a decent mechanic."

"If he is Muslim, he will be honest."

"That's not necessarily true."

"Yes it is! A real Muslim would never cheat another Muslim. He will cheat the *kuffar*, maybe, but he will never cheat another Muslim."

"If someone is dishonest, then he's dishonest. I think you're making a mistake."

"I don't care what you think!"

I was annoyed at my mom for throwing her money away on this shoddy car from a shady salesman when there was a perfectly decent Volvo for sale from a reputable dealership. It was about $500 more, but at least it was guaranteed to run!

Usually when my mom and I fought about something, I would concede to her wise judgment because I just didn't trust my own. This time, however, I was sure I was right. That had *never* happened before. It was a weird feeling. In college, I was developing my critical thinking skills—I was using my brain in a way it had never been used before. This was new and exciting and I craved more and more. I loved hypothesizing, testing out different angles and perspectives, then arriving at a conclusion. It was so invigorating! I was so used to being told what to do and how to do it that this newfound skill of discovering what I should do was intoxicating. I decided to dip my toe into the possibility that I might be right and that my mother might be wrong.

It was her money, and she was free to buy whatever she wanted. I stopped giving her my advice. In fact, I encouraged her to go ahead and buy from the shady Muslim.

I would stand back and see if she was right or if I was right. If she was right, I would continue to submit to her judgment. If I was right, then I would know that I could actually trust my own judgment and, in fact, it could even be more sound than hers!

Well, the car flat-out died after two days on the road, and the dealer refused to give her her money back. He would only offer to "fix it." And it would die again a few days later. The car ended up being such a hazard—it kept dying in the middle of traffic—that she finally gave up.

That was a defining moment for me. I had tested my hypothesis, and it turned out that I was right. This opened up a whole new world in my mind. It was indisputable evidence that I could trust my own judgment, my gut, and my ability to make sound decisions.

At the end of the second semester of my first year in university, I was writing a psych exam when I suddenly realized I couldn't form a complete sentence. The answers swam around in my brain, but there was no way I could get them out onto the page. I had never felt such a disconnect between my body and my brain before. I had been burning the candle at both ends for so long, I was no longer getting even my four hours of sleep per night, and I was severely sleep-deprived. On top of that, I'd been getting sick, and my body was struggling to fight off a virus. But I was a single mom going to university full-time, plus I was tutoring in the evenings, I couldn't afford to get sick. So I popped antihistamines and pain relievers in dangerous amounts to ward off my symptoms. But they kept coming, so I chased the pills with some NeoCitran, a cough suppressant and decongestant. I never had the time (or money) to eat on campus, and I was generally too rushed or too tired to pack myself something before leaving the house. Long story short, no food, plus pills, plus NeoCitran, plus crushing stress, equals not good.

I was so frustrated and scared that I did something I had not done for a long time, not since everything backfired with Mr. Fabbro. I asked for help.

Clutching my exam in my sweaty palms, I walked carefully up to the instructor. I focused very hard on forming the words to try and explain my situation. I expected her to tell me to suck it up, sit down, and write the exam or submit it as is. I expected her to tell me off for thinking I might get some sympathy or preferential treatment from her.

"NeoCitran," I said. I must have looked pretty awful because her first reaction was a very breathy "oh" followed by wide eyes and outstretched arms. I remember she wrote *NeoCitran* at the top of my exam. I could tell from her eyes that I could stop stressing. She was going to let me go! She handed me her card and told me to contact her to see about making up the exam. I had never felt such utter relief. I went from desperation to salvation in less than a minute and burst into tears. Not sobbing, just tears streaming down my face. I managed to thank her, even though the lump in my throat seared with pain. I slipped out of class and got on the next bus home.

Later when I met her in her office, I was struck by how kind she was. *Kuffar* are supposed to hate me. I was taught that they were my enemy and that they were to be mistrusted. But she showed me a compassion that brings tears to my eyes all these years later. My own mother had never looked at me with eyes so kind.

She commented that I seemed to be overburdened, possibly depressed but definitely stressed. I told her that I was going through a lot, and that I was struggling immensely. I told her of how I clenched my teeth so hard in the night that I would wake up in pain that would last all day. She recommended I go to counselling to ease the pressure. Since she was a psych instructor, I asked if she could be my therapist. She explained it wasn't her role and tried to suggest alternatives for me, but I panicked. I had found one person willing to be nice to me and help me—what were the odds that I would find another? I told her I only wanted to speak to her because I trusted her and simply could not trust anyone else.

I can't imagine how desperate I must have seemed. In hindsight, I was clearly suffering from depression and anxiety and a lot of other things, I'm sure. I think she knew that if she didn't agree to see me, I would not seek help elsewhere. And she would have been right, I wouldn't have.

I was so grateful that she agreed to see me that I insisted on paying her the going hourly rate for psychologists, about $100 per hour. She finally accepted, but she told me that she'd only be able to see me for a few sessions. I handed over the cheque after our third meeting, knowing I couldn't afford to see her again. I stressed so much over making sure enough money was in the account to cover the cheque. A few weeks later, though, I realized that she had no intention of cashing it. I had met my third *kafir* angel. First my lawyer, then the cashier at the supermarket, and now my psych instructor.

I wanted to go back and talk with her more, but I couldn't bring myself to take advantage of her kindness. I knew she would still refuse to cash the cheques, so I had to stop seeing her. Instead, I decided I would honour her generosity by following through with the life lessons she had taught me. To this day, she has no idea how much she changed my life.

I'd spoken with her about my desire to move out from under my mother's iron fist. After explaining all the reasons I wanted to and all the reasons I should, I ended with, "But, I can't."

"Why not?" she'd ask.

"Because I can't. Women can't move out on their own. You live either with your family or with your husband. Women can never live alone. I can't bring that kind of shame on my mom. I can't."

"Imagine you can't say *can't*."

Who knew what a profound effect those words would have on my life? Maybe she knew, but I didn't know. What a turning point! It's how everyone must have felt when they discovered the Earth wasn't flat.

The possibility that there was even a possibility that there was something beyond *can't* had never even occurred to me. And now, there I was staring at a horizon that didn't actually end. In that same psych class, we had learned about baby elephants who are tied to massive slabs of concrete from birth. Those little babies fight with everything in them to get free, but they can't. Their legs bleed as they cry and struggle, but the concrete doesn't budge. Eventually, the baby elephant realizes it can't get free, so it accepts its fate. And because an elephant never forgets, you see grown elephants that could move a truck with their tusk if they felt like it attached by a rope on their leg to a teeny tiny bolt in the ground. They accepted their fate long ago. They stop trying because they believe they can't. If only those elephants knew that if they made the slightest deliberate tug, they would be free.

I was one of those elephants.

That was the first time I realized that I was the only one standing in my own way. I had to get past the fear that had been burned into my brain. They all wanted me to believe that I couldn't make it on my own, and I had believed them. But, oh, the sudden delicious knowledge that I could! And they didn't know that I knew! They thought I still believed! They walk away and leave me attached to that bolt believing I won't ever yank it out. They go to sleep in their beds confident that they have me convinced I am weak. But I had the upper hand. I knew I was strong!

I let this knowledge settle and permeate and grow in me as I went about my life as normal. I was very scared, but I trudged forward despite the fear. Surely Allah would not burn me in Hell for eternity just because I was trying to save my baby from the same life that I had lived? He would have to understand that I needed to get her out of that toxic environment, away from my brother and mother. I would explain it all to Allah, he would understand. I knew I would get a chance eventually, but I had to wait for my window of opportunity. I couldn't arouse suspicion by making any sudden moves.

Not too long after my private revelation, my mom started to make plans to go visit my sister in Florida. This was my chance!

One of my friends had a neighbour who was building an illegal basement suite. He needed to rent it out quietly and under the table. Perfect! I had zero credit or references, so I wasn't going to be able to rent a place on the up-and-up, anyway. Plus I would get to live near my friend! So I quietly planned it all out. When my mom was in Florida, I would pack my daughter and our bags, and we'd get the hell out of Dodge! And that's exactly what happened—without a single glitch. She left, I packed, and we moved out.

FREEDOM

It was just a basement suite, but it felt like a magical paradise of freedom. Freedom that came at a very high price, but it was worth every single penny. My suite wasn't much to look at—you could see 95 percent of the suite from the front door—but to me, it was priceless. I remember commenting to a friend that I would gladly pay even more rent than the asking! No price was too high for liberty.

If you took a few steps from the front door and crossed through the living room/bedroom and then the kitchen, you'd find the bathroom to your right and my daughter's bedroom ahead of you. In there I put her bed, a dresser, and a toy box. I never had my own bedroom at her age, so I was ecstatic to be able to give her a bedroom of her very own. I got stickers for her wall and a colourful duvet. I doted on that room, as it represented the very first step in my healing. Giving my daughter the things that I never had was so fulfilling, I no longer grieved or ached over missed opportunities. Giving all those opportunities to her healed me, that little girl inside of me who had been betrayed, forgotten, and ignored. I couldn't make it up to her, so I tried instead to focus on my new little girl. I wanted her life to be everything mine hadn't been.

We lived in that one-bedroom suite for about a year; those months were a journey of self-discovery. My daughter went to a day care that was walking distance away. I no longer relied on my mother for anything. No more childcare, no more financial support, nothing. It was me and my baby against the world. And nothing was going to stop us.

One of my biggest concerns was trying to figure out how to be a mother. I decided that the best course of action would be to do everything exactly the opposite of what my mother had done. She raised us to value death and the afterlife and to not to give any credence to this world. So I did the opposite. I taught my daughter to enjoy every moment, to find the happiness in every breath. Before going to bed at night, every night, she would tell me three things she was thankful for. Anything from the fact that it was a sunny day to being thankful she had a yummy cupcake in her lunch. Later, when she got older, she started keeping a gratitude journal. She's grown up now, and she still keeps one. Discovering how to raise a small human life back then was not easy, but when I look at her today, I realize I did something right.

Those weren't easy years. We moved around a lot, always chasing a cheaper rent. My aim in those days was to get my affairs together as quickly as possible so that my daughter would never remember a time when we didn't have money for food or when we lived in a bachelor apartment and shared a futon. I didn't want her to remember this version of me. I wanted to be a role model she could be proud of.

By my calculations, I figured I had until she turned six. That's when my clear memories started. She was already three, so I didn't have much time. But I was on the right trajectory. I worked so hard, so fast, so much, I would barely sleep, and I sustained that for years. I knew that I would make my deadline. I had no other choice. I went to school full-time and worked, and I was even able to start loving, positive relationships with new friends.

As Dickens said, "It was the best of times, it was the worst of times." I had my freedom, and nothing was better than that. But I also had to deal with something I knew nothing about: life. Up until then, I'd always been told what to do. Critical thinking, decision-making, forethought—these were all foreign concepts to me. I was taught to listen and to obey, not to think. Suddenly I had to figure everything out. How would I get to school every day? How would I pay for day care? The decisions to be made were endless. I often messed up.

I remember sweating bullets as I dropped old Egyptian coins as bus fare (it went by weight), so I could get to school. I was running out of money. I had to take three buses between my home and the university, so obviously I didn't live in the best location geographically, but it was the best financially.

I did the whole Egyptian coins thing until they were all gone. Then there were those days when I walked my daughter to day care only to have to go back home and cry. I didn't have enough money for bus fare. If I had friends over and bought extra food, that was all it took.

I would get so angry at myself because school was my ticket. If I didn't do well in school, I would never achieve my goal. That anger and sadness, and being consumed by the sense of failure and fear, propelled me to make sure those days of missing school were few and far between.

But when my daughter asked for an overpriced box of frozen waffles and I said no because I just didn't have the money, I felt even worse than I did for missing school. I was failing the one person I'd aimed to please. That was my first rock bottom.

I scrambled to the surface again, cursing the fact that frozen waffles were so expensive, and managed to get back to where I was before—skipping like a pebble on the surface of the water, terrified I'd sink again and never get up. I was filled with adrenaline. I knew I couldn't stop. If I even slowed down, I would fall into that water and drown. I had to keep moving, but it was so hard. The hardest day was the day I had to sell my grandmother's bracelet.

After my grandfather died in a boating accident, my grandmother moved from Saudi Arabia to Montreal. Because they were non-Saudis living in Saudi Arabia, all of their properties and their businesses had to be cosigned by a bona fide Saudi, because foreigners are not allowed to own anything in Saudi Arabia. Once my grandfather died, the cosigning Saudi stole everything and left my grandmother with nothing. She had no choice but to move in with her son, my dad. I went to Montreal to visit her about two years after my grandfather's death.

She was very frail, and her eyes were clouded over with glaucoma. Although she was still relatively young, it was clear she wouldn't live much longer. Living with my dad and his horrible wife had taken its toll on her. He had pushed her against a wall and broken her arm, and then he refused to take her to the doctor, accusing her of whining and lying that her arm hurt.

She was tired of living. She and my grandfather had been together since she was twelve years old and he was fifteen. He'd been a big burly man with a big laugh and a big personality. Every now and then she'd have to endure him slapping her on her bottom or giving her exaggeratedly loud kisses, but mostly she just sat quietly at his side. Without him next to her, she was lost.

We sat on my dad's couch, and she cried as she pried the last remaining gold bangle off her wrist. She always had half a dozen jangling on her, but now there was just one left.

"I'm sorry it's not new. I hate to give you something old and scratched, but it's all I have. I want you to always wear it," she said handing it to me. "Remember me when I'm gone."

"No, please. Keep it. Don't talk like that. I don't need something to remember you. Where are you going? Don't say things like that."

But she insisted. And I only took it so she would stop crying. I vowed to never take it off. I kept my promise for as long as I could. The bracelet was the last thing of value I had. I sold it to cover the cost of rent, tuition, and food. I suppose that was the true rock bottom. I can't think of a lower point in my life.

That same year, I received a $3,000 grant from my university. No more bus fare problems; I would finally be able to get a car. Relief flooded through me.

I was too scared to spend it all on a used car, though, because I had no idea how to deal with any mechanical issues. I opted for a lease instead.

At the dealership, which was walking distance from my house, I tried to convince the salesman to lease me a car.

"You have to understand," he said. "You have no credit, and you're a full-time student. You don't have a steady income. You're a very high risk. The bank will never agree."

"I promise I will pay every payment on time. I will take such good care of it. You have to believe me." My gut was churning as if I were on a roller coaster.

"They will only agree if you pay a $3,000 deposit and get someone to cosign. Do you have anyone that could cosign with you?"

"No. I have no one." And my stomach churned harder.

"No mother or father, aunts or uncles? Anyone in your life with credit?"

"I guess I could ask my dad. I haven't spoken to him in years."

"Try that," he said. "Here, you can use my phone."

"It's long distance; he's in Montreal."

"It's okay, go ahead."

He pointed to the phone and then walked out to give me some privacy. I took a big breath and dialed. When my dad picked up, I told him the whole story. He was less than enthused that I would intrude on his life to annoy him with my problems.

"You know you can't just call me out of the blue asking for money."

"I don't need money—just your signature." I could hear his tight sigh of exasperation all the way from Montreal.

"You know, it's essentially the same thing. If you do not make your payments, I will be left on the hook, and I have three children to support. I have a wife. I have mortgage payments. I am not a bank for you."

"A bank for me? What have you ever paid for? Did you even pay child support? I really don't think you're being fair," I said. I could hardly believe the words were coming out of my mouth. "I've never asked you for anything, and this is barely even asking you for anything, and you still can't do it? You can't just sign a piece of paper for me?" I was in tears. "You don't have three children. You have six children. Remember? What have you ever done for me as I was growing up all those years? I never had a father like your new kids have a father!"

He was my last chance. If he didn't agree, I wouldn't be able to get the car.

I felt like throwing up as I got flashbacks of standing in the rain with my daughter at bus stops, watching thousands of commuters speed by.

"Mommy, look! There are so many cars!" she would say. "And look!" she'd exclaim, pointing at a full parking lot. "There are so many everywhere! Why can't we have just one?"

"I promise I will get us a car, my love; I promise."

And now I wouldn't be able to keep my promise.

The salesman walked in and saw me sobbing into his phone. I thought he was going to offer to cosign it himself. He looked as bad as I felt.

"Daddy, please. I won't ever miss a payment, I promise. You have to believe me. I don't know what else I can say. I need this car. I have never asked you for anything, and I will never ask you again."

"My wife won't like it. We already have a lot of bills."

I could not give less of a flying fuck about your wife.

"She'll never know unless I miss a payment, and I won't. I promise. Please."

After multiple pleas from me and copious guidelines from him, he begrudgingly agreed to sign. I got my car, and I treated it better than any car had ever been treated. I never missed a single payment in the three years I had it. After the lease was over, I paid $200 to get the car fully detailed, and the dealer said he'd never seen a car returned in such perfect condition before. I was very grateful that that dealership took a risk on me, and I was determined to repay their kindness.

DOUBT

As I got more comfortable in my new life, I randomly chose an elective that fit into my schedule—History of Religions. It focused on the three Abrahamic religions, and since I'd had Islamic studies rammed down my throat for as long as I could remember, I knew that at least one third of the curriculum would be a breeze. I had no idea how much that course would change my life.

During those twelve weeks, everything I knew about everything slowly unravelled. I had never looked at Islam from an objective perspective before. I could now see the absurdities in it just as clearly as I could see the absurdities in other religions. It was easy to see the irrationality in the trinity or in revering cows, but when that irrationality is your own, it's harder to recognize.

For the first time, I was allowed to look at Islam with a critical eye, and I quickly discovered that the Quran was no different from any other ancient philosophy, no different from any other book written by men. It was so glaringly obvious. With reference to the Earth being as flat as a carpet or to the value of drinking camel urine to cure ailments, Islam was full of absurdities. It was obvious that it was written by men who knew no different. I had the revelation that it was not the divine word of some almighty deity. An almighty deity that created Heaven and Earth would know that he didn't create it flat!

As well, this notion that the Quran was special and divine was proven false as most of it had been (badly) plagiarized. There are even many instances where foreign languages like Hebrew or Syriac ended up in the Arabic printing. We were told, of course, that those were words with mysterious meanings that only Allah could decipher. But, no. It's just a bad job of plagiarism. The Quran was cobbled together from the teachings and tales told by Jewish and Christian tribal leaders.

I finally came to accept that not only was Islam made up, but in fact all religion was made up. I was ecstatic to finally let go of the crippling guilt I'd carried for years! I didn't have to feel inferior because I didn't believe in these nonsensical and oddly violent fairy tales—I had been the sane one all along!

What a relief to finally be able to breathe fresh guilt-free air! I wanted to get drunk and go clubbing and do all of the things that single free women do!

It would not be that easy, though. Just like I hadn't immediately shed the niqab and hijab, I didn't immediately shed all of the indoctrination that was pummelled into me from the age of five. It's extremely traumatic to suddenly realize that everything you thought to be true is a lie. I felt like Jim Carrey in *The Truman Show*. The onslaught of emotional turmoil—anger that I was duped, sadness that I wasted all those years, fear that I might be wrong, embarrassment that I was that stupid—was nonstop. But through that process, there were times when I would decide not to think too hard and just embrace the freedom.

Luckily, I had a gorgeous friend named Tosha to be my Sherpa in this world of newfound freedom. She knew everything there was to know about hair and makeup, and I was her dutiful student. We'd spend all week in classes together, working our butts off, then on the weekends she'd dress me up and we'd go clubbing, and it was glorious! I was finally busting out and shaking off the last remnants of my concrete prison and experiencing life in a way that I never imagined I ever could.

Not only was Tosha my hair and makeup mentor, she also helped me grow up in general. Her parents were going through a divorce, and she had just discovered something very poignant that she shared with me, that I have shared with numerous people since.

"You know, your mom is just a woman," she said. "She's just a woman like you and me and all other women. We put our moms up on this ridiculous pedestal. We see them as different from the rest of humanity. But they're not. They're just women."

We were in her car, and her words pierced me like a chisel cracking off the largest remaining chunk of cement that covered me. I just stared out the windshield trying to process what she was saying. When we reached my destination, I hopped out automatically without a word of reply—I have since told her how grateful I am. That statement of fact made such a profound difference in my outlook. My mother—and my fear of her—was the final piece that I needed to overcome. And Tosha helped me to overcome it.

Islam attributes almost deity-like status to mothers. They get to decide whether you burn in Hell for eternity. That's pretty powerful. But to recognize that, no, she does not possess any supernatural powers—that she's just a lowly, sinning human like the rest of us—was quite a mind-blowing insight.

I didn't live with my mom anymore, but I was still deathly afraid of her finding out that I was taking off the hijab part-time. I was living a double life. In the evening, I didn't wear my hijab, but I kept it on at school because I didn't want to deal with the questions. It was post 9/11 now, and everyone was acutely aware of people in hijab.

My mother, predictably, only mourned for the Muslims who were killed in the twin towers.

"You know there was a day care in there," I said.

"Well, sometimes there are casualties in war."

"That's not a war. That's an attack on innocent civilians."

"Don't be stupid. Muslims are always at war with *kuffar*. That's your problem, you never understood that. And that's why you'll probably be killed with them. When you live among them, then you will be indistinguishable, and for that you will deserve what you get."

"You live among them, too."

"Not like you! I do not have *kafir* friends! I hate them and their country, and I will go home as soon as I can! You love it here! You love them! You think you are one of them! But you will have no choice but to join the Caliphate when we succeed in overpowering them, or you will be killed with them like a dog."

My mother's view of the world was no different than that of the 9/11 hijackers, no different than that of ISIS. They all believed that it is a Muslim's duty to fight until all people are Muslim and all of the planet is ruled by Islamic Law. It is the reason why when the Caliphate rose in Iraq and Syria (ISIS), Muslims from all over the planet flew over to join the fight. It made no sense that young men and women from Western countries were choosing to go to a war-zone, people could not understand it. But it made perfect sense. Like me, those people were taught, from when they were children, that it is their duty to support an Islamic state. Once ISIS gained power, the recruits were already indoctrinated and ready to join. They did not see themselves as terrorists, they saw themselves as fulfilling a divine plan.

After 9/11, smugness and celebration were the kinds of attitudes I would get from the Muslim side of my life. Meanwhile on the *kafir* side, the polar opposite was happening.

The Dean of my faculty called me down to his office to ask me if I had dealt with any backlash. Muslims had just killed thousands of

Americans, and his first concern was that no one was making me feel uncomfortable. Oh Canada! If you only knew what you were dealing with and how strange your concern seemed to me. No, no one had made me feel uncomfortable. In fact, they were going out of their way to make sure that I was always comfortable. I felt like asking the Dean, "Seriously, are you *kidding* me? We're calling for your death, and you're concerned that our feelings might be hurt?"

It was nauseating and condescending, to be honest. I was not a special little snowflake that needed extra attention because people who shared the same religion as me were murderers. The whole thing was ridiculous. The immediate concern should be dealing with the trauma of all our lives being different now, and that there was no going back. We could no longer feel safe. The heart of our world had just been attacked. Everyone was struggling to make sense of it. Everyone was in a state of shock.

I resented being connected to those monsters in any way. I hated that this fucking cloth on my head made me look like I was complicit in that shit. I was just as terrified of the terrorists as everyone else. My life was as shaken up as everyone else's. My heart broke for all the victims, just like everyone else's. There were no other layers.

I wanted, more than anything, to rip off that cloth and remove any connection between them and me. But removing the hijab, when I was already under a microscope, was not an option. Pre-9/11, people probably wouldn't have even cared, but there was no going back to our pre-9/11 world. I imagined if I showed up one day without it on, I would get *way* more attention than I was comfortable with, and I was already getting way more than I wanted. I imagined people would ask me if I was still Muslim, and how would I answer that? I was still grappling with that question myself.

They might even take my hijab-less state to mean that they can talk about the filthy "sandniggers" around me, as I had clearly denounced the religion, so naturally I must hate all Muslims. And, of course, I didn't want them ever misconstruing my personal journey out of faith as an invitation to be hateful to those still in it. I wanted to avoid putting myself in the awkward situation of having to defend my position and reasoning because I still had not actually defined my position or reasoning. So, because of the messiness surrounding the decision to commit in one way or the other, I was a hijabi by day and a free spirit by night.

To the world, I looked like a Muslim woman. But on the inside, I was just a woman. I was slowly losing my identity as a Muslim, but I hadn't yet discovered what I would replace that identity with. I was rolling with the punches of life, taking it day by day, and trying to straddle life bouncing between two identities.

That's when I got the call from my mom to turn on the news. There was a BBC correspondent standing in the middle of rubble in an Al Qaeda safe house in Kabul, and papers were flying all around him. The reporter reached down, grabbed a random paper, and read it on the air.

"This one says 4U Enterprises. Richmond, BC, Canada. Now, we don't know what this company is or if it is of any relevance, but . . ."

Out of all the papers that he could have picked up, *that* was the one? What were the odds?

It didn't take them long to find me. My answering machine was full.

"Hi there, I'm calling from the *National Post*. I wanted to speak to you about your ex-husband's company, 4U Enterprises. Could you please give me a call back?"

The callers were relentless. Eventually, they started camping out in front of my building, waiting for me to leave. I felt violated and scared. Why was *that* world intruding into my new world? It had nothing to do with me. One of the reporters made it up to my door.

"Do you have a moment to talk about your ex-husband?"

"No! Leave me alone! I don't want to talk to anyone! I don't know anything about him! Please, leave me alone!"

"We won't leave you alone until you talk to us. If you just talk to one of us, then the rest of us will go away. We just need a statement."

"I have no statement."

"Look, take my card and call me when you're ready to talk. Your phone won't stop ringing, and we won't move away from your building until you do."

His threat left me no choice but to angrily oblige. I just wanted them gone. It felt so weird for them to be involving me in events I was not a part of. None of it had anything to do with me. After our phone conversation, my story was on the front page of our national paper. And, as promised, they all left me alone after that.

As I walked into school the next day, my professor pulled me aside and spoke to me as if I were some kind of celebrity.

"Is this *you?*" he gushed. "I can't believe you're in my class! It said you were a student at UBC, so I just thought, well, what are the odds? And it was you!"

"Yeah, I don't really want to talk about it." I pulled away from him.

"Well, this whole thing is absolutely fascinating!"

I kept on walking.

The article contained a lot of information that was new to me. It revealed that an Al Qaeda operative, who had been arrested on terror-related charges, was the one who posted Essam's bail when he was arrested upon entering Canada with a false Saudi passport. In great detail, it described how this operative was instructed to withdraw money from an account in California and pass it on to another Al Qaeda operative in BC.

The men, who all identified as jihadists, said that this jihadi mission to free Essam was based on direct instructions from Osama bin Laden. The article mentioned that Essam had been involved with bin Laden since the Soviet war in Afghanistan. They believed he was the person who trained the bombers responsible for the 1998 bombings of the US embassies in Kenya and Tanzania that killed over two hundred people.

When I told him I was going to divorce him and he left Canada, he went to fight with the Serbs in Kosovo. But about a year later he was caught in Azerbaijan and sent to prison in Egypt. And that's the photo CSIS had shown me years ago.

I had hoped that was the end of that chapter of my life. I was moving on, and I really did not want this to haunt me for the rest of my days.

I was only a bit nervous when Morsi, an Egyptian president for a short time after Mubarak, let a group of Muslim Brotherhood operatives out of prison. The truth is that Essam hated the Brotherhood; he thought Islamists were a bunch of pansies. He was actually aligned with a more militant group in Egypt called Al Jihad, who were the Egyptian wing of Al Qaeda. Both Islamists and jihadis have the same goal—to spread Islam, but they have different methods. Islamists want to do this through passive means such as politics, immigration, and childbirth. However, jihadis prefer the method used by the first Muslims: the sword. There is a hadith in which Mohammed says that the best Muslims are his generation, and then Muslims get successively weaker as time goes by. So naturally, the current generation of Muslims is always the worst generation. Muslims should never allow Islam to progress; they should always strive to emulate what Mohammed and his companions did 1,400 years ago. That is why jihadis consider Islamists to be less religious, less pure, American sellouts who trim their beards and wear suits. True Muslims dress like the prophet and act like him, too. With Morsi being an Islamist, he would prefer to keep jihadis like Essam behind bars. They may have the same goals, but they are not allies.

I like to think that Essam's most likely dead now. And any friends or allies that he had, who would be willing to hurt us for him, are hopefully dead, too. He'd be about sixty now. His prison sentence was for fifteen years hard labour, so he could be out now, but it's highly unlikely his body would be very strong after such a lengthy stint in an Egyptian prison. I can at least rest easy that he would not be a physical threat to us. I can't imagine the Canadian government would ever let him back in. I learned from a *New York Times* article online that he was the contact point for bin Laden's terrorist cell in Canada, so he'd most likely have trouble travelling back here. I keep checking to see if his Wikipedia page has been updated; one day I will read confirmation that he is actually dead.

REBUILDING

As difficult as it was financially, I had some good times in those years of dismantling my Muslim self, and rebuilding myself brick by brick. I'd have my childhood friends over and we'd do one another's hair and makeup and play music and dance—all the things forbidden in our families' homes—and just be free twenty-something girls. My place was so popular for that.

These girls were still stuck at home (one was stuck in a loveless arranged marriage), and my place was where they could be free. The friend who had helped me get the basement suite had a brother who had a best friend named Wayne. One time, as my friends and I were hanging out, Wayne came over unannounced. In those days, I still wore a hijab, so he had never seen my hair before. I don't think he was expecting me to look quite so different; I could see he was visibly taken aback. I giggled and ran away, uncomfortable with the attention. Later, my friends would not let it go.

"The . . . the way he looked at you!"

"Yeah, well, I guess he thought I was bald."

"But none of us were wearing hijab! He didn't even glance at us. It's like we weren't even there! He only saw you!"

There was truth to what they were saying, and it was flattering. But friends always exaggerate such things. So I was really surprised when he came back later that evening and made it abundantly clear that he was looking for more than friendship. My head was spinning. As much as the idea thrilled me, it also terrified me.

I had taken the step to move out, but having a boyfriend was a whole new step. Having a relationship with a member of the opposite sex—especially a non-Muslim one—was strictly forbidden. Not only was there literally Hell to pay once you were dead, on Earth it was also potentially dangerous. The shame and guilt were debilitating.

When we first started sleeping together, I freaked out so much that I almost gave myself a panic attack each time. To calm my nerves, I would imagine that we were married. I would imagine that he was the hateful, violent, horrible man I was married to—and that would be calming! I was so afraid of having sex with a man I wasn't married to that I would imagine I was actually with a man who I *didn't* want to be with in order to get through it. The brainwashing had a truly insidious hold on me: Wayne was *haram*; Essam was *halal*. Even though I wanted to be with Wayne and hated Essam, I could only calm down enough to have sex with Wayne by fantasizing about Essam—if you could even call it that. That is truly messed up.

I struggled tremendously with the thought of having a non-Muslim boy in my life. Men are allowed to have non-Muslim partners, but women are only allowed to have Muslim partners. I was breaking so many cardinal rules!

But it was wonderful to be able to have someone to rely on, to have a comforting hand to hold, to have a warm hug at the end of a hard day. Wayne was completely harmless, and he loved me. And there was such a comfort in knowing that he loved me more than I loved him. That gave me the control. I never feared that he would ever hurt me.

"I would do anything in this world just to see a smile on that beautiful face."

How could someone be saying those words to *me*? It was all so surreal. His words were like a healing elixir to a person who was so sick, a person who had no idea what healthy even felt like.

I fought against the feelings of guilt and fear and let the relationship happen naturally. We never really announced that we were a couple, but he was always just there.

As the years went by, we went from being friends, to being friends with benefits, to eventually getting married. We didn't have a wedding, just a quick civil ceremony in the courthouse. I think I mostly got married to alleviate all the guilt I was feeling for sleeping with him. If we got married, it would absolve me of my past sins.

He met my mom once, but only after he said his *shahada* and became a Muslim.

"What if they ask me questions?"

"They won't. Just repeat the phrase after the Imam."

It took him ten seconds to become a Muslim. He was willing to jump in, learn all about it, and do anything I wanted.

"I won't eat pork!"

"Eat all the pork you want, babe, please," I said. "I appreciate you doing this for me. I won't ask you to do any more."

All I wanted was for him to mumble the words "There is no Allah but Allah, and Muhammed is the messenger of Allah" in front of an Imam so that my mom wouldn't be hateful toward us.

I didn't tell him that the punishment for apostasy was death. I didn't tell him a lot of things. There was no need for him to know as I was pretty much on my last thread of believing in those days, anyway. I knew it was just for show.

I was teaching at an Islamic school, though, so I still had to wear hijab by day, but that was all just for show, too. I was still living a double life. Now, instead of wearing it by day at school, I was wearing it by day at work.

At least at home I could be myself. Quite often I would rip off my hijab in the car on the drive home. My daughter, in the back seat, would do the same. Ever since she was just in kindergarten, she was required to wear one as well.

I know a lot of ex-Muslims who live this double life and live with their parents! I can't imagine what that would be like. It's one thing to endure when you're brainwashed, but being forced to live like that once your mind is free? That's hard to fathom. It must be torture.

But everyone has their own shade of suffering. None of us can make this transition easily. It is a struggle that all ex-Muslims share. We call it being *in the closet* as the term fits our predicament as well.

Once I quit the Islamic school and started teaching at a college, I had no reason to keep up the charade. Everyone in my life knew that I didn't wear the hijab anymore—except for my mom. I didn't really think through how I would tell her. Our relationship was hanging by a thread now, anyway, and I suspected this might be the last straw. To be honest, I would have been relieved if it were. I just wanted to live my life freely. I didn't want to put up any pretenses for anyone anymore. I was tired of living a double life. And if that meant she'd disown me, so be it. It's not like I felt I'd had a real mother, anyway.

I barely saw her, as we lived separate lives with multiple cities in between us, but one day she called me up to ask for a ride to a doctor's appointment. With courage and confidence, which I had gained from my History of Religions course, my mind-blowing insight from Tosha, and the realization that my mom had no control over me—and that I would be fine without her—I decided that I would walk out the door as I would any other day.

"Are you sure . . .?" Wayne was excited but worried. "Do you want me to come with you?"

"No. That might make it worse. This has to happen eventually. Today is as good a day as any other."

I took a hijab with me and left it in the back seat just in case I lost my nerve at the last minute. I almost did. But I willed myself to keep driving without stopping, not giving myself a chance to put it on. When I pulled over to pick her up, she opened the car door, took one look at me, and started screeching.

"Why are you naked? What is wrong with you? I am not getting in the car with you naked like a whore! How are you not ashamed of yourself walking around like that? *Aouthoubillah! Astaghfirullah!* I am so disgusted with you naked like an animal! How dare you?"

I responded in a very calm and low tone. "Do you want a ride to the doctor or not?"

"I am not getting in the car with you, you filthy prostitute!"

"OK, then please shut the door so I can go home." To my surprise, she actually got into the car. But her constant stream of insults did not cease.

"Curse you! Curse you to Hell! You will be burned! I will never allow you to even smell paradise! You deserve to suffer for eternity. You should be killed! If we were in Egypt, I would have you killed! I should kill you with my bare hands! So are you a *kafir* now? Have you lost your religion completely? Are you a filthy *kafir* now?"

"No. I just don't want to wear the hijab anymore."

"Of course not! Because you're a slut! Only filthy whores want to walk around naked displaying their body for every man to lust over!

You are disgusting! I should kill you and bury you in the backyard! Oh the shame, the shame. You better not come to my funeral! I am not your mother. You are nothing to me. You are dead. I wish you were dead. How could you do this to me?"

When her shrieking ceased, she became somber. Her voice came out steady and determined.

"I won't risk leaving you alive to leave Islam. I will kill you before that happens. You will not drag me down to Hell with you."

She believed that she needed to kill me to save her soul. According to her religion, she saw no other choice. If she raised a daughter who became an apostate, then she would be punished for eternity. It would be her fault. Allah would punish her for it. She had to kill me to make sure that never happened.

I was not surprised by her conclusion. I had expected it. But just like when I married Essam, hoping against hope that he might end up being a decent person after all, I had hoped that my mom wouldn't reach this inevitable conclusion. It made sense. My wants, needs, happiness, or even safety never superseded the religion before—not from when I was six years old being beaten for not praying—so why would things suddenly be different now? The edicts of the religion always took precedent. The demands of Allah were always paramount to anything else.

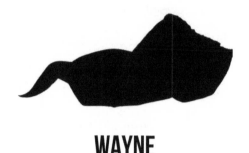

WAYNE

After dropping her off that day, I never saw her again. That was in 2004. I had phoned her a couple of times since then from a safe, undisclosed distance. But not long after that dreadful day, I finally had to accept that there was no point in trying to keep the relationship. I was no longer interested in her approval; I had grown past that. And that was the entire basis of our relationship. Her withholding love until I did her bidding, and me doing everything I could for her approval. That cycle was broken now, as I accepted that no matter what I did, it would never be enough. There was no point at which she would grant me the love and acceptance I so desperately strived for. Even marrying the man she chose, living as a ghost of a human with no sense of self, could not satiate her.

I had decided that I would live life for my own happiness, not hers. It made me sad that her happiness caused me misery and my happiness caused her misery, but there was nothing I could do about that. I had one life. One chance on this planet. I was not about to squander it living for anyone else's happiness but my own.

It had no effect on our day-to-day lives, as she was barely in our lives anyway, but it did feel a bit like a death had occurred—the death of what could have been, I suppose. I had tried doing it her way, I was unwilling to wallow in muck for all my days for the promise of Heaven. Heaven didn't even sound enticing; it sounded stupid. Heaven was conjured up to entice a male brain. For women, it sounded boring. Besides, I didn't believe in any of those imaginary motivational carrots anymore. I was only guaranteed the breath I was taking. Carpe diem!

It took me quite a few years to fully get over the fact that she would never call. She would never accept me as I was. She would never be the mother I wanted her to be. I had no choice but to accept that I truly was dead to her, and in turn, she was dead to me.

But life went on. Wayne, my daughter and I moved into a gorgeous new house. We bought all new furniture together. We had two cars. From the outside it looked like we had it all.

Wayne was accommodating and agreeable about everything. He was fine going along with anything I wanted.

I remember sitting there, admonishing myself for not feeling happy. What else could I possibly want? I had all the things that society says you need for happiness. But for some reason, it just wasn't enough. I had been through too much, and I was exhausted. But, somehow, settling for mediocre made it all for naught.

When we met, we were both in a transitional period of our lives. I was moving away from being a Muslim under my mother's rule to becoming an independent woman, mother, and student, making it all on my own.

He had just lost his mother to cancer the year before we met. I think we both needed the stability that marriage would offer. We both craved the family environment that was missing from our lives.

We offered that to each other, but we could not offer much more. In every other way, we were a bad match. Pop psychology would tell us that we are each the youngest sibling, so neither of us was open to steering the ship. And there's definitely an element of truth to that. He was looking for a mommy figure, and I was looking for a strong partner to care for me and help me to create a stable, family environment for myself and my daughter. I didn't want someone else to take care of.

As the three of us were sitting down to breakfast near the end of our very short marriage, I started to spread jam on my piece of toast.

"Can I have half?' my daughter asked.

"Sure," I said.

"Can I have the other half?" Wayne asked.

For a fraction of a second I paused, then I handed him the other half. I had just experienced my life in a nutshell. That was exactly it. As long as I stayed with him, that would be my life. I would be ever giving and never receiving.

I learned so much from Wayne. I learned that I was worth loving. I learned what it was like to be in a loving relationship. I learned that I could keep breaking barriers and defying Allah and nothing would happen! Even though I no longer believed in all the nonsense, the fear and doubt that maybe I was wrong would creep in now and then. But I'd had premarital sex, the ultimate sin for a woman, and I was still in one piece! I learned that I had married him because he was safe and secure, and I was vulnerable and broken. I learned that he was great for me at the time, and I am grateful that we could be there for each other when we each needed the other. I cannot honestly say that I was ever *in* love with him, but I definitely loved him. That's not good enough to sustain a marriage, though.

It was scary divorcing him. I had just lost everything, including my identity. He had filled a huge gaping void for me, but I knew I would never love him the way he wanted me to. I married the first boy who saw my hair and found me attractive. Chances were I would meet other boys—and I could choose one who would make me toast, not one who would take mine.

DOHA

The year before I turned thirty, I accepted a teaching position at a college in the Middle East. In Doha, Qatar—a country I had never heard of. I was scared of making any decisions in my life, but this one was particularly big and scary. This was the first time that I was relying exclusively on my own judgment and ability to make sound decisions. And if I messed up, I would be messing up my daughter's life as well.

The second Iraq war was at a fever pitch. I was petrified that I was making the wrong decision. I decided to phone my mom and tell her about my decision. She took the opportunity to tell me what an irresponsible mother I was for taking my child into a war zone, where we could be killed by the *kuffar*. I regretted my decision to call her. She only made me feel worse.

I had to accept the position. It offered a great salary and housing, utilities, furniture, and appliances would all be paid for by my employer. I would get generous vacation time, plus the cost of a trip home every year. I would be able to pay off my student loans, provide a life for my daughter that I had envisioned, and likely even be able to come back home with enough money for a down payment on a house! How could I resist?

I listened to Gloria Gaynor's "I Will Survive," Frank Sinatra's "My Way," and Eminem's "Lose Yourself" on repeat to get myself pumped. "Faith" by George Michael and "Get the Party Started" by Pink were also on that CD mix.

I had to remain calm and focused—to swallow all doubt. I had to do this. I had been through so much. I told myself this would be a walk in the park in comparison.

The only thing of genuine concern was that I would be living in a Muslim country. I had Wayne's last name, and I didn't really look Arab. The only concern was my first name, but I figured I could just say that my mom was Egyptian—Coptic Christian. My name was Arabic, but not Islamic. I could get away with not ever mentioning that I was ever Muslim.

The thing was that although I didn't really believe in Islam anymore, I still hadn't identified what I did believe. I went through quite a few stages. First, I was a nonpractising Muslim, then I didn't believe in any organized religion, then I was spiritual but not religious, then I was agnostic, and then finally I identified as atheist. Eventually, I discovered the term *ex-Muslim*, but that came years later. Throughout that transition, I wholeheartedly believed I was the only one to have ever gone through any of this. I had never heard of, or knew of, any Muslim who had left Islam. It just wasn't an option. It's a part of your identity. It's almost like choosing not to be Black anymore. Well, you can't. It's just who you are.

It took me years to discover and understand that "Muslim" was not an identity. Islam is an ideology that you choose to follow or not. If you choose not to follow it, it comes with a death sentence, of course, but the point here is that it was not an innate part of me! I *could* shed it! And I did.

Before I did, however, I had to go through many, many learning experiences. It was a dark, winding, and very lonely path. These days, ex-Muslims have social media to support and guide them—the path is still dark and winding, but at least it's not as lonely.

It's strange, now, to read about how common it is for an ex-Muslim to say, "I thought I was the only one." Again, I had thought I was the only one too, but millions of others were and are thinking the same thing—that they, too, felt they were the only ones.

Islam isolates you like that. It is like a school of fish all moving in one direction, and if you don't fall in line, you feel ostracized and different. You're told in a thousand little ways that you're broken, so filled with the devil, you need to be fixed or saved. It's shameful. You feel like such a pariah. How could you even think of sharing your impure thoughts with anyone?

It's all part of the genius and insidious methodology of keeping all the *ummah* in line. How can you control individuals? Turn them into mindless drones. Manipulate their minds from a young age so they truly believe there really is just one path. That is what they are told every day from the moment they can comprehend the meaning of words.

I was engulfed by this school of fish not long after landing in Qatar. In fact, it was during the very first orientation session. A woman in hijab, all excited, came running up to me as I walked out of a bathroom stall.

"Your name is Yasmine! Are you Arab?"

"Sort of, my mother is Egyptian." I should have just said no.

"Ooh, *ahlan wa sahlan*! I'm Egyptian, too!"

Suddenly, I was surrounded by a swarm of women oohing and aahing over me. I tried to nudge past them to wash my hands.

"*Ahlan beeki!*" I responded. Instantly, I felt like a moron.

"Ooh, you speak Arabic! Did you ever live in Egypt? Where did you live? Are you from Cairo? It's so exciting to meet you! We get together to belly dance every Friday, do you want to come? Do you like Amr Diab? Do you know who he is?"

I was positively suffocating as I tried to inch my way from the paper towels to the exit. These women were just trying to be friendly, but I found them to be incredibly invasive, and I was terrified.

I didn't want people to get wind of the fact that I was, or rather had been, a Muslim. I was living in a country governed by Sharia. The punishment for apostasy was death. There were no ifs, ands, or buts about it. This is the most dangerous part about Islam today: Sharia.

There are no other theocratic nations in the world except for the countries under Islamic law, including, of course, the fifty-seven countries that are members of the Organisation of Islamic Cooperation. That is scary. As long as those countries are following Islamic laws, they will *never* progress beyond seventh-century barbaric, misogynistic, and homophobic laws. People can be free to believe in all the sky daddies and fairy tales they choose to believe in, but they cannot impose the musings of their imaginary friends on others—at least not in a modern democracy.

Having been born in a secular, liberal democracy, I had no idea what I was getting myself into. And it's a good thing, too. If I had fully comprehended the extent of the danger I was putting myself and my daughter into, I never would have gone.

I was not going to be protected by secular laws or religious freedom here. Under Sharia, if you leave Islam, you get your head chopped off. End of discussion.

As I was trying not to hyperventilate and just slip out of there without answering any of their questions, a colleague walked in. She worked in HR, her name was Jennifer, and I had just heard her speak in the orientation session. I knew nothing about her, but the sight of her allowed the oxygen to reach my lungs again. I stretched my hand to her instinctively, like you would if you were drowning in a pool and you see a shadow above you.

"Are you okay?" she asked as she took my hand.

"No. I don't feel well. I think I need water."

"Ooh." The gaggle of women dispersed and let me through.

As my colleague walked me toward the drinking fountain, she chatted calmly about the desert heat, how it can reach upward of 50 degrees Celsius, and how I needed to be careful to stay hydrated. I interrupted her to tell her that the truth was I was extremely uncomfortable with the women in the bathroom.

"What did they do to make you uncomfortable?"

"I don't know."

What could I say? I didn't want those women to get in trouble just for being friendly, but at the same time I needed a reset button. I didn't want them to know I was part Egyptian. I didn't want them thinking I was one of them. I couldn't get caught up in that mess. I was too scared that the truth of my background might come out involuntarily. I couldn't be around them. I babbled incoherently, not saying anything, really, and eventually my colleague let it go.

"Okay, I'll talk to them."

"They were just being nice," I said. "I don't want them to get in trouble."

"No, it's okay. I understand."

But how could she understand? She must have thought I was crazy.

After that I was careful to never divulge that I understood Arabic, to never utter a word of Arabic, and to never volunteer the fact that I was half Egyptian—unless it was to a Canadian colleague, of course. And even with them, I was cautious about how much information I divulged.

Luckily, in comparison to Arab countries, obsession with identity is pretty much nonexistent in multicultural Canada. Most Canadians don't really care to know anything about your past:

"What part of Canada are you from?"

"Vancouver."

"Okay, great."

Done. Moving on.

If that were an Arab, it would be a twenty-minute conversation to extract everything about my ethnic, religious, and specific geographical background so as to ensure that they were pigeonholing me with all the respective stereotypes and assumptions. I was familiar with this all-encompassing fishbowl life. I remembered it from my time in Egypt. I instantly had a physical aversion to going back to living like that again. Not all of the world has a caste system, but it might as well.

So much was happening so fast. I was starting a new job in a new country and living in a new home. My daughter was starting a new school. Everything was chaos. And on top of it all, I was going through a divorce. At one point while unpacking the groceries, I collapsed at the sight of a jam jar.

My daughter preferred Wayne's peanut butter and jam sandwiches to mine because he would always get the ratio magically right.

After crying on the kitchen floor with a jar of jam in my arms and the fridge door left wide open, I got up, dusted myself off, and continued putting away the groceries. There was no time to harp on the past. No time to deal with it. I had to keep going. That was the way all tragedies had been dealt with my whole life; that's what I was taught. And that's pretty much the way I conducted my life until I decided to sit down and start writing this book.

Everything came to a crashing halt a few months later when a car bomb blew up the local theatre. The theatre was just for expats. It was full of British, American, Australian, and Canadian people. I had tickets to go to that night's performance, but I had bailed because my daughter wasn't feeling well.

The Egyptian who drove the car into the building died on impact. Everyone in the theatre was able to escape when they heard the huge bang. Once they were all out, the director went back in to make sure everyone had been evacuated, and that's when the bomb went off. The Director did not survive.

It was a day that hit me as hard as 9/11 did.

I seriously considered packing up and going back home. But back where? Wayne and I were no longer together. I couldn't go back to living with my mom. At least here I had a house and a job. I had to make it work. I decided to give it one more chance, hoping I wouldn't live to regret that decision. If anything else happened, I would be on the first plane back home.

I developed a nervous tick in my right eye that didn't go away for six months. Other than that one time in university when my arm got paralyzed right before an exam, and the occasional panic attack, I had managed to avoid any physical manifestations of my stress. The tick scared me, but I just ignored it and kept moving forward.

No other terrorist attacks happened, and I started to relax and enjoy my new life. It was a strange new opportunity to wipe the slate of my life clean. No one in Qatar knew me or anything about me. I could reinvent myself in any way I wanted. By that point, I had successfully dismantled all of my Muslim identity. So now it was time to rebuild from scratch. It was an opportunity people rarely get—an opportunity I took full advantage of.

I could now finally be a true feminist, not a confused and constantly apologetic Muslim feminist. I didn't have to make excuses for why Allah gives a girl half the inheritance her brother gets or why in a court of Sharia a woman's testimony is worth half of a man's or why Mohammed said women are deficient in intelligence. I could happily denounce all that misogyny without feeling scared that I might be punished in some afterlife. I could proudly say to myself and my daughter, you are worthy. You are second to none.

Unfortunately, I was in a country where everything in society was in complete disagreement with my new unapologetic feminist attitude. I looked around at a sea of black—no woman discernable from another. All shrouded, erased. It is a place where feminism is yet to take root. No one, not even the women, are willing to entertain the idea that they are equal members of society because it contradicts the religion they hold so dear. Seeing those women and interacting with students, I knew that this could be the string to pull. I knew that the women rotting under those suffocating sheaths were starving for freedom, for autonomy—at least some of them were. It was human nature. They could only lie to themselves so much. Cognitive dissonance only goes so far, then you're left to face the point where reality and your imagination intersect. If women are Queens in Islam, if Mohammed was the first feminist, then why can't I divorce my abusive husband? The religion allows him to beat me, to rape me, and does not allow me to divorce him. Trapped women would recognize their captor. I wanted them all to find their freedom and happiness like I did. I trusted that they would eventually rise. I just hoped to be alive to witness it.

As much as I wanted to reach out and support those women then, I was preoccupied with my own upheaval. It was not an easy life. Living under a theocracy, I was always tense because I never knew what could happen. I was acutely aware that I was not at home. I was on their land, and with any misstep they could kick me out at a moment's notice. This was especially nerve-racking because I had a child. It wasn't until two years after I was back on Canadian soil that I fully released the tension I didn't even realize I was holding on to.

In Qatar, everything was dictated, starting with your place in the racial hierarchy: Qatari Arabs at the pinnacle, followed by Whites (American, Canadian, Australian, Brits), other Arabs (Lebanese, Egyptian, Syrian, etc.), then people from the Philippines, and finally, at the bottom, people from South Asia (Indian, Pakistani, Bengali, etc.). What you wear is dictated, especially for women, as is what you eat, what you drink, where you go, and where you live. You have your place in that society. And if you want to live in Qatar, you need to know your place.

I hated it, but I also loved it. I loved the close friendships. I loved that my student loans were dwindling. I loved that I could travel. I was being pushed to try new things. I was being pushed to allow my daughter to try new things. She had a best friend who had an eccentric mother who was always pushing boundaries. When the girls were just seven, she ganged up on me, with the kids, to let our daughters go on a roller coaster. Not only was I afraid of roller coasters, I was especially afraid of a roller coaster in a developing country with little to no safety standards! I finally gave in but then felt sick. I spent the entire time they were on the ride crying uncontrollably until I had my daughter in my arms again. That summer, those same girls went bungee jumping in Thailand! I was really getting pushed out of my comfort zone.

That first year was really difficult. The best part was when Tiffany came to visit me.

"It's like this place was built by Dr. Seuss. Nothing makes sense and everything is so weird," Tiffany said as her first impression of Doha.

I caught her crying as she was watching TV one day.

"What's wrong?"

"Look!" she exclaimed. "Trees!" For someone from the west coast of Canada, living in the barren desert of Qatar was akin to living on the moon.

"What the fuck is that?" she enquired on a different day.

"What? Where?"

"Are those whales?"

And then I heard it.

"Aaaaaaaalllllllllaaaaahhhhhhhhhhhuuuuu . . ."

I realized she was talking about the long, drawn out nasal whine of the call to prayer! Since I heard it five times a day, I just tuned it out, but it was an eerie and strange sound for Tiffany.

They say to fake it till you make it. Well, I faked it. I was a college instructor. I was smart. I was confident. I was a strong woman. I was the only woman strong enough to be a single mom in such a misogynistic society. I became the woman that I wanted to be. I became her so well that at one point I realized I wasn't faking it anymore. I was her. I'd conjured up exactly who I wanted to be, and I was her. I first realized this when the Dean of my faculty made a comment after observing my class.

"You're so confident. And you have every reason to be. You're an excellent instructor,"

"Confident?"

I completely skipped over the compliment on my teaching ability. This was the first time anyone had ever described me as confident! Had I finished faking it? Had I made it?

"I don't feel confident at all. But thank you."

Gaining my confidence took about a year and was not an easy process, but it was definitely facilitated by being one of the very few single women in a country *full* of single men. Most of the men were disgusting perverts who came from countries where it was perfectly acceptable to leer at women. I thought the men in Egypt were bad—the men from the Indian subcontinent and South Asia were all much, much worse. But at least they kept their distance. None of them would ever dare speak to me, so I just avoided eye contact and kept my distance.

The Arabs, however, were something else. They thought that because they were rich, all women would be interested in them. It boggled their minds to learn otherwise. I even had fellow expat women question me.

"But you're so lucky! You're everything they want! You're like their ultimate woman! You have the right hair, the right complexion, the right face—you could bag yourself any Sheikh you wanted!"

"Too bad I'm not interested in any Sheikhs."

"What a waste! If I were you, I wouldn't miss the opportunity."

Well, Little Miss Clueless didn't know what she was getting herself into. All she saw were dollar signs, but I understood the real price she would be paying.

To be honest, I wasn't interested in finding a man. In fact, I actively worked at being single. The men in the Western expat community were all very helpful with boosting my ego. I had never felt so beautiful and desired as I did in those days. It was very healing to have that kind of attention to counter all the negativity of the past. The cutest boys in town were flocking to me and vying for my attention! It was a surreal but welcome change.

In my first year there, I got into a relationship with a coworker. By the time that year was over, I had transitioned into a different woman from the one he had initially been attracted to. I was no longer the nervous, unsure woman who was slowly rebuilding her life. I was now the woman I wanted to be: the woman who would be a role model for her daughter. In the beginning, I was fine with his temper tantrums, but not anymore. Now, I knew I deserved better.

LOVE

My second year began very differently. I was fully confident and secure in my new identity. I was completely established as the woman I had always wanted to be. I was ready to take on the world. I wanted to finally embrace life as a single woman. I wanted to be like Ally McBeal or one of the women from *Sex and the City*!

Not long after the new year began, I bumped into the love of my life.

I didn't want to love him. I didn't want to love anyone. I refused his advances over and over again because I didn't want a man ruining my cool single-girl vibe. But at the same time I was afraid that if I didn't see where this relationship would go, I might regret it for the rest of my life. I didn't think I would ever meet anyone like him again. I knew there was something different about him. We had an inexplicable connection that I couldn't deny, even though I tried.

Every time I turned him down, he'd just be all sweet and tell me he'd rather be friends with me than not have me in his life at all. He always knew exactly what to say and do. I have no idea how he did it. I would find reasons our relationship wouldn't work, and by the time I would see him again, he'd have eradicated whatever it was—even if I hadn't said anything! He just instinctively knew.

We had this bond that was so immediate and so undeniable, regardless of how many times I pulled away, it was as if he just wouldn't humour me. He ignored all my skittishness and just continued being amazing to me. He effortlessly rolled with the punches and jumped through all the hoops. I was so used to being logical and factual and ignoring my heart and feelings—it was the only way I could survive. But he was making me want to listen to my heart. I had to go through therapy to learn to trust again. And, eventually, I let him in. I let go of all my fear, anxiety, and trust issues, and just let myself fall in love.

This was the first time in my life I had ever been in a loving relationship, the first time I knew what it felt like to be truly in love and truly loved. It took me a while to recognize this strange feeling overcoming me: happiness. The tightness in my chest loosened, the hotness in my blood cooled, I was high up in the clouds living a dream that was so much more magical than I could have ever conjured up.

And then he hurt me. For a regular couple, it might have been easier to get over these things, but I was not a regular girl. I had known nothing but heartache and pain and suffering and toil, and this was the first time in my life I actually believed that I might get the chance at something different. I had trusted him. I had believed him. I really did think I was worthy of all this love and adoration. But now my inner demons rose to challenge me. *How stupid of me to be so naive! I never should have allowed myself to be vulnerable. And, of course, as predictably as everyone else in my life, he hurt me.*

They say opposites attract, and that was definitely true in our case. He had lived a charmed life. He was clueless as to what real struggle was. The word *stress* was nothing more than an intangible concept. He had no idea what it felt like. Meanwhile, I had no idea what it felt like to *not* be stressed. In the ten years before we met, he had spent his time travelling around Europe without a care in the world—a stark contrast to how I had spent the previous ten years.

We were from two completely different worlds. If we hadn't met in the Middle East, most likely our paths would never have crossed in Canada. We were from opposite coasts of the country, with thousands of miles in between us. Not just geographically, but in every way possible. We were yin and yang.

But there's something about opposing forces that create a symbiotic relationship. His lack of stress was the exact antidote to my life of nothing but stress. His carefree, live-in-the-moment attitude was exactly the remedy for my constant worry about the future.

He taught me to spend a lot of money on good food (*But it'll just end up in the toilet in an hour! What a waste!*). He taught me to travel (*But what if an emergency happens and we're far from home?*). I was like

Chicken Little, and he was *so* goddamn sure that the sky wasn't falling. And I wanted to believe him.

So I fought for us. I don't think he'll ever appreciate how much I fought for us. He can never know what it was like for me or how much it took from me to be able to trust him again.

And the truth is that years into the relationship, even after we were married, had a baby, and had moved back to Canada, I still didn't fully trust him. There was always a piece of my heart I kept from him, a piece that stayed strong in case I ever needed to break free. I kept a close eye on the finances and was careful to calculate what I would need to continue on my own if I ever needed to kick him out. I would never let go again. Fool me once . . .

I didn't actually get over it until I immaturely, and very dangerously, hurt him back. I'm so glad he fought hard for us that time. The tables were turned, and he proved to me that he was wholeheartedly committed to me and to our marriage and to our family. That was his final test, and he passed with exuberantly flying colours!

For our ten-year anniversary, we went back to Vegas, where we were initially married, to renew our vows, but this time it was Elvis who officiated. Finally, I can say with conviction, I let go of that one little piece of my heart that I was harbouring for safety. I no longer constantly calculate our finances to ensure that I could take my girls and flee at a moment's notice. I finally don't have one foot out the door. I finally feel safe enough to get in the house and shut the door behind me. I never thought I would get here. It wasn't even a realistic goal, as I didn't think it was attainable, and I thought it would be supremely unwise.

In hindsight, I think I was just so overwhelmed with happiness and love that I forgot life is not a fairy tale. I went from one extreme to another. My life was not a horror story anymore, but nor was it a fairy tale, either. I've learned that life is a comfortable safe haven right in between.

I do love him, and I never thought I could ever feel this kind of love for another human being who I didn't give birth to. He has a huge heart, and he instinctively is everything I need, even when he doesn't understand why. He is my reward for surviving all the trauma of my past and persevering. He is my light at the end of the tunnel.

I think what made me hold on through the ups and downs was Tiffany's voice. She liked him. And I trusted her judgment more than my own. About a year after our marriage, Tiffany went in for routine tests, but she never made it out of the hospital. She had a congenital heart defect that was a result of her mother being prescribed a derivative of thalidomide when she was pregnant. Tiffany's heart was like a patchwork quilt, and only her cardiologist understood how it was put together. Her doctor was away when Tiffany went in for the screening. She was injected with a dye so the doctors could see how it travelled through her arteries. There was a complication during the CT scan that she'd had dozens of times before, but this time her doctor wasn't there.

To say I was devastated would be a laughable understatement. I honestly felt like I was no longer connected to this planet. Tiffany was the only person who remained with me from my past to my transition into the woman I am today. We lost touch over a few years when I was married to Essam, but I found her as soon after my escape as I could. She was my only life witness. Without her, did I even still exist? Tiffany passed in the month of her birthday—November. So now I fall into a deep dark depression every year between Halloween and Christmas. It's unfortunate that both of my daughters have their birthdays between those times. I have to force myself to plan parties and make costumes and buy presents and put up decorations, when the only thought that gives me comfort is the thought of ending my life. It's the only thought that feels right, that makes sense. I remind myself that I have to just fight the urge until spring. But it's exhausting. And I fear one of these dark winters I just won't have the energy to fight anymore.

But I plow through life as I always have. When things are not dark, they are glorious. I am so grateful for every sunny day and every breath. I am so grateful for my husband and for my daughters.

We have a smart, caring, funny, gorgeous and all-around amazing little daughter together. She further heals me as her sister does. She gets to be raised in a stable, loving home. She has a wonderful big sister who dotes on her and adores her. She excels in anything and everything—soccer, piano, hip-hop dancing, learning languages. She's got every opportunity a child could desire, and she does not squander any of it. I would do anything to protect her unscarred life. She is what we all have the potential to be if we are not marred by the grown-ups in our lives.

Neither my husband nor my youngest daughter will ever meet my mother. I have not had any contact with her since 2004. At first my pain was so deep that it would immediately be usurped by my anger, becoming almost indistinguishable from it and, ultimately, inextricably bound to it. But no one can live like that forever. Now I just feel numb. It took an incredibly long time, but finally, honestly and truly, I no longer even care what happens to her. I was done wanting her approval a long time ago, but then I was left with this indignant need for her to apologize and accept and take responsibility for all the pain she caused me.

I am so thankful to say that I am finally over all of that. I do not want or need anything from her.

Because my mom is the matriarch of the family, I have no contact with my siblings or other family members, either. I had a brief encounter with my brother when about ten years after I had discovered it, he discovered that my mother was hateful and manipulative. But because of all the years of being estranged, and all the trauma and anger and resentment, that reconnection was short lived.

I am now quick to sever toxic ties. I don't waste time forgiving and trying again and again as I used to. So when my sister accused me of lying about being abused by her ex-father-in-law/ex-stepdad, I cut off contact with her. She's so far down the Islamic rabbit hole, anyway, that our worlds are not even in neighbouring universes. Both her daughters (one slightly older than my daughter, and one younger) are married already, and her son is attending one of Canada's top universities. That familiar cycle continued unhindered.

I have one uncle who I speak to periodically; he raised me when I was a baby while my mom went back to work—from infancy until I was about one or two years old. So we had a special bond. He calls me Jesse. It's a mystery why he chose that nickname, but I love it. And I love him. Since 2004, he has been my only extended family. I've had no contact with anyone else.

Then one day my uncle mentioned that I had a cousin (her father was my mother's half brother) who was estranged from the family because she married a Jewish man. Well! I immediately contacted her and told her that I, too, was a misfit and that I hoped we could meet up. She answered me right away and then came to visit me soon after. It was so glorious to meet another ex-Muslim family member! I can't explain how lucky I feel to have a family member in my life who loves and understands me fully. I am so grateful that my daughters get an Aunt.

I am sad that I wasn't born into a loving family, but I am certainly not alone in that. A lot of people grow up with rotten parents, but they still turn out to be very successful human beings. I am not as sad as ex-Muslims I know who loved their parents and who grew up in happy homes. To be discarded by your father for renouncing your religion when you had been daddy's little girl has got to hurt them a lot more. My dad barely knew me. To be discarded by a mom who you admired, a mom who was there for you to hug away every hurt—that must be supremely more painful. Though it was unfathomably lonely and scary to sever ties, it was the less painful option for me. I was willing to pay the price for a chance at a better life for myself, and, more importantly, for my babies.

I am sad that I have no baby pictures of my older daughter. Her father forbade pictures, and it took me a few years after escaping to be able to afford a camera. Her face is etched in my mind, though. My precious girl. I spent so many hours studying her face as I promised her that she would have a good life. That she would know happiness. That she would know freedom.

I am sad that my daughters will never know any of the Egyptian side of their family. None of that means anything to them. Talk of Egypt might as well be talk of Greece or China; they're all just faraway lands.

Neither of my girls speaks or understands Arabic.

Neither of them will ever fear being burned by an invisible man in the sky if they don't bow to him five times a day.

Neither of them will know what it's like to feel ashamed of their bodies or of their hair.

Neither of them will be forced to do anything they are uncomfortable doing for the sake of an arrogant and vengeful figment of a seventh-century goat herder's imagination, ever.

Neither of them will ever have to overcome child abuse, whether psychological, physical, or sexual.

I have been able to protect my girls, and for that I am grateful. I have succeeded in my life's mission. I broke through the cement that entombed me, and I stopped the cycle. All the subjugation, humiliation and indoctrination dies with me.

I was the bridge; I was the first generation—I was Hodor from *Game of Thrones*, holding the door so my daughters could live free. They won't know any of the life I've lived. It is as foreign to them as it is to some of you. So I am happy. I am a success story. I persevered. I refused to submit.

FIGHTING BACK

Writing this book was a difficult yet rewarding journey. It was difficult for obvious reasons; I don't think I have ever cried in my whole life as much as I did while writing this. I was forced to go back into dark memories that were deeply buried. I threw off the covers and let all the monsters out from under the bed. All these experiences that I had never shared with my friends, my husband, and didn't even allow myself to acknowledge—I have written out for the whole world to read.

It was rewarding and cathartic, as you'd expect, to release all those demons. Once the light shines on them, they're not so scary anymore. I had a writing professor once tell us that we swallow the saliva in our own mouths unconsciously all the time, but if we were to spit on our desks, we'd never lick it up and swallow it again. A crude way of putting it, but it drove the point home. Once you let something out, it's not the same anymore. And, most importantly, it's not in you anymore. And thank goodness for that!

It was also rewarding because of all the wonderful people I have met online! I wish I could gather you all in a huge bear hug. Posting on my Tumblr blog, my Facebook page, and on Twitter has allowed me to connect with so many amazing, gracious, kind, and loving people. I really could only get through this because of your encouragement and support. Every time I got a message, whether from an old high school friend, a closeted ex-Muslim woman in Saudi, or the child of one of my work colleagues, it was like a fresh shot of oxygen that gave me the energy to plow through.

There were many times when I just couldn't bear the thought of sitting down to write again, of 'going into the darkness' as I started to call it. But that's when I'd find a note in one of my inboxes with a heartfelt message from someone who could relate or who was writing to express their gratitude or appreciation. So that's why I continued. I wanted to be brave for you all. I heard you cheering me on from all over the world! From France, Iceland, Italy, Poland, Egypt, Iran, Pakistan to name just a few, and from my own backyard in the United States and Canada. Your cheers meant the world to me, and they still do. I know I could not have done it without you.

I know this is my unique story, but my story is not unique. Since going public, I have been bombarded with messages from women and men relating to my story. I tried my best to support each person. I knew they did not have anyone in their life they could trust, but they trusted me—that was an honour and a responsibility that I did not take lightly.

I took it so seriously, in fact, that it almost killed me. There was no reprieve. And I was not a professional. I had no way of separating myself from the stories I was hearing. I felt like each one of those people were my children. Meanwhile, my actual children were being pushed to the back burner. Once in the middle of my daughter's soccer game, I got a Skype call from Somalia, and I felt I had to take it. I knew it was from a girl who was worried about her father identifying her as a person who left Islam to the local terrorist group, Al-Shabab. She would have the choice to repent and return to Islam in three days or be killed. Surely this was more important than watching my daughter score some goals?

But eventually it all came crashing down around me. I broke. It crept up on me and then hit me like a ton of bricks. I found myself unable to function without persistent, debilitating panic attacks that were always lurking. I told my husband that I felt like a thin tissue blowing in a rainstorm, trying to avoid the drops of rain. I knew something significant had to change.

I tried to find a professional who I could refer all these people to. A professional who would understand the predicament of these ex-Muslims stuck in Muslim-majority countries, where the state-sanctioned punishment for leaving the religion is execution. I had been to many counsellors who gave advice like *talk to your mother*, and *maybe you can work it out*; laughably simple advice that would not at all work in this context. If these people talked to their mother, they could get killed. As I was searching, I came across Jimmy Bangash, an ex-Muslim of Pakistani descent living in the UK who was disowned by his family because he was gay. He was a life coach going to grad school to get a master's degree in counselling psychology. He was a perfect match. Immediately, I started up Free Hearts Free Minds (FHFM) and started sending clients to him. It was the perfect solution. I could now get professional help for the people who were contacting me. We prioritize women in Saudi Arabia and members of the LGBT community, but we help as many people as we can. If you visit our website, you can read testimonials from some people we have helped. It is such a rewarding organization to be a part of. We run on donations only, and every penny goes to supporting people and saving lives. Please visit our website to read more and, hopefully, to make a donation—www.FreeHeartsFreeMinds.com

As well as the gratifying work at FHFM, I am rewarded every day by the women who use hashtag #FreeFromHijab. One woman who I had been privately messaging with (as she did not fit our FHFM criteria since she was in Canada, not in a Muslim-majority country) was struggling a lot with questioning her faith. She decided that on #NoHijabDay, she would remove her hijab on camera for the first time. Her video went viral. She made a statement about women's emancipation in Arabic, English, and French, then removed her hijab. The video ends with her beaming smile. Her video got so much attention that the cheering of the crowd encouraged her to take it a step further and leave her abusive husband, too! Her freedom began with removing the hijab, but that was just the first step. Now she is entirely free—her body and her mind! That is the power of social media. People think clicking "like" or "Retweet" won't do much when in reality it can literally transform lives. I see it happen every day.

I see women in Saudi Arabia, Egypt, Iran, Algeria, Yemen, Sudan and other Muslim-majority countries who are encouraged by the cheering masses online demand their autonomy. I see women hiding their face, then showing their hair but still covering their face, and then eventually showing their whole beautiful self proudly! It is such an incredible honour to be a part of that. As a kindergarten teacher in Egypt, I felt so rewarded that every word in English those children would ever read going forward was because of me. Working with these women now, I get the same high. To be involved in encouraging women to liberate themselves, to live freely, is the best possible use of my life.

HOPE

The day may be approaching when the whole world will recognize woman as the equal of man. ~ ***Susan B. Anthony***

Susan B. Anthony said those words 135 years ago. Unfortunately, the day she predicted has not yet come to pass.

In the United States 135 years ago, women were considered the property of their fathers and then their husbands. Their clothing was dictated for them as were the jobs they could have and the person they would marry. Over the past century, women have fought for emancipation through first wave, second wave, third wave, and now fourth wave feminism. As admirable as those waves are, they barely register as ripples outside of the Western world.

Western women may well be recognized as equals of men, but in many parts of the world, brave suffragettes, counterparts to Susan B. Anthony, are still fiercely fighting for their equality.

A deep disconnect exists between the feminists in the Western countries and the feminists in the Muslim-majority countries. Growing up as a first-generation Canadian in a fundamentalist Muslim family, I spent a lot of time being caught between those two worlds.

At home I was taught that from the time I was nine years old, I needed to wear a hijab to protect myself from men who wanted to molest me. From my society, I learned that this is called victim blaming.

At home I was taught that good, pure, clean girls wore hijab, and filthy, loose, despicable girls did not. From my society, I learned that was called slut shaming.

Given the choice between those two worlds, I eventually chose to break free. That decision almost cost me my life and my daughter's life. But it was a risk I was willing to take, not only for me, but especially for my daughter.

As a young girl, I grew up reading about historical heroines of the suffragette movement. The small minority of freedom-fighting women faced imprisonment, risked their lives, or even willingly gave their lives to bring attention to their plight. These were women who were on the outskirts of society. They were disrupting the status quo. They were a threat to order. Not only did men find them threatening, as their cause was in direct resistance to the male-dominated society, but women were threatened by them as well. Those women were my heroes. I wanted nothing more than to be as courageous as they had been.

And now as an adult woman, I work with suffragettes like them every day from all over the world. Like me, these women have seen both worlds and are choosing to risk their lives for the chance to live as free women. They are women in Iran who get lashed and imprisoned for refusing to wear a Sharia government-mandated cloth on their heads. They are women in Saudi Arabia who are tortured in prison for demanding the right to drive a car or to travel without a male guardian's permission. They are young girls in Afghanistan who are shot in the head because they want to attend school. They are little girls in Sudan who burn themselves because they do not want to be married off. They are young women in Egypt fighting to keep their bodies intact, unmutilated by razors.

I don't have to refer to a history book to find women who are risking their lives to fight societies that view women as second-class citizens. I interact with them every day. Yet, tragically, most prominent Western feminists are not standing alongside me and these brave freedom-fighting women.

Many feminists in the Western world are afraid that by supporting their fellow sisters, someone might misconstrue that as ethnocentrism or racism. And even worse than just ignoring them, at times Western corporations actively support the very things that these brave women fight against. The 2019 swimsuit issue of *Sports Illustrated* featured a burkini. And most egregious, the poster for the Women's March depicts a woman in hijab.

Feminists in America would never cheer Nike for putting a swoosh on Mormon underwear, yet they cheer for it being put on religiously prescribed modesty clothing from a different religion. How can we fight

Western patriarchy while simultaneously supporting Islamic patriarchy? I hope this book has dispelled all the myths and confusion that lead to such hypocritical and dangerous disconnects. People in Muslim majority countries are just trying to progress their culture in the same way Western culture have. You have been able to abolish slavery. You have been able to fight for women's equality. We just want to do the same. Why is it that when we try to progress, suddenly it's a bad thing? We get called Islamophobic for criticizing Sharia and pushing for change. Why should we have to retain our misogynist, homophobic cultures? Cultures are not sacred—they are dynamic. They are meant to be changed with human progress. That is not a bad thing. It was not a bad thing for you and it is not a bad thing for us.

Apartheid would not have been abolished from South Africa without the pressure from the international community, the Berlin wall would not have fallen, slavery would not have been abolished—humanity's greatest social achievements can be realized only if the strong turn around to lend a hand to those in need of support. I survived the darkness and clawed my way into the light. Now that I am here, I feel compelled to reach my hand back to help other women achieve their freedom. I want to help turn those burgeoning ripples of feminism into waves that will resonate across the rest of the world.

The Muslim world has been shielded from criticism for so long. How will progress ever happen if criticism is considered bigotry? Ironically, the same man who screeched that criticizing Islam was gross and racist had no issue with making a movie that mocked Christianity. Why wasn't that gross and racist? Why is this condescending attitude only reserved for the religion of the "little brown savages?" Is it bigotry of low expectations? Are Muslims not entitled to go through enlightenment and reform just as Christians have? Didn't that happen because of people criticizing the Church? Didn't that criticism eventually lead to the separation of Church and state? How can that happen in the Muslim world when there are people with this patriarchal attitude shielding Muslims from progress? Could they not see that Ben Affleck was the one who was truly gross and racist? Could they not see that he was the one who was using a different yardstick depending on the ethnicity of the people?

I hope I have gotten my message across. I hope that people will start to assess one another and deal with one another based on ideas and not identities. I hope that when people meet a girl being beaten by her family, they won't bow down to the ethnicity of her parents. I hope they will realize that all little girls bruise, regardless of ethnicity. I hope they understand that justifying the beating because of the ethnicity of her parents will condemn her to a life of physical and psychological torture that will stay with her until the day she dies, regardless of the colour of her skin. I hope they will choose to protect the child rather than a faceless, nameless culture or religion that is undeserving of protection. Religious rights cannot supersede human rights. I hope they will understand that doing so is not only gross and racist, it is inhumane.

I hope that when you're around the water cooler at work or on a random Facebook page, you will share your honest thoughts and not be bullied into silence. Blasphemy laws in Islamic countries force people there to stay quiet. If we also choose to be quiet because of self-imposed blasphemy laws, who will be left to speak? It is our responsibility and our duty and our privilege to speak our minds. People have died so that you and I can have the right to free speech. What a dishonour to their memory if we squander this gift they have given us.

I also hope you choose to speak up for women—all women. Throughout my life I have watched things improve for women almost daily. It was not a drastic change born through bra-burning or other protests; it was a slow change as we all shifted and manoeuvred ourselves around this recognition that women are equal members of society.

I've watched significant changes happen in media—as movies, commercials, and music videos started avoiding sexist stereotypes and allowing women to have roles with depth and breadth. I watched Sheryl Sandberg rise to prominence with her book *Lean In.* I learned from her and from Oprah Winfrey and from Michelle Obama and from Beyoncé and from countless other women in popular culture who are examples for young women growing up in North America. As Geena Davis asserts in the documentary *Miss Representation*, "You cannot be what you cannot see." But I could see. I could see a lot of women who I regarded as heroes.

I think a lot of young women, the generation after me, saw these heroes as well. And like me, they wanted to join the fight. They, too, wanted to be an example, an inspiration, and to continue to pave the road that had been laid by the brave women before us. But unlike the women before us who had to tear down old-growth, thousand-year-old trees and build new roads one pavestone at a time, these young women were born into a world where there were bulldozers at the ready, willing to support them in their endeavour. The work was happening, the fight had essentially been won. We didn't need to convince anyone that there needed to be roads to equality—everyone was already on board.

But these young women wanted to build roads too! Since most roads had already been paved, these young women, so full of energy, exerted their efforts in different directions. They began to discuss whether we should start calling ourselves womxn, if air conditioner settings in the workplace are sexist, and how to counter the social phenomenon known as manspreading. With no legitimate problems to overcome, they invented problems so they could fulfill their desire to solve them.

If only those young women knew that there is a way to travel back in time, to link hands with the history-making heroines who had risked their lives to fight for freedom. There is a way they could channel their energy into supporting women who just want to be regarded as equal human beings to the men in their societies. There is a way they could support girls who just want to go to school without fear that they might be shot in the head. There is a way they could help girls who don't want to be married off as children. All of these issues, and so many more, are right under their nose. And we don't need a DeLorean to go centuries back in time to find these women. They exist today. Women who get arrested and disappear because they dare to take a scarf off their head in Iran. Women who are arrested and disappear because they drive a car in Saudi Arabia. Women who are arrested or killed for showing their face and hair on social media in Pakistan or Iraq. Those brave women exist all around us, and they want nothing more than to be supported by feminists in the West.

Imagine if Susan B. Anthony and all the other suffragettes were alive today, but instead of helping them in their emancipation, you chose to ignore them because you were afraid that supporting them might be misconstrued as bigotry or racism? Or worse. What if you chose to support the people who wanted to keep these brave women down? Unfortunately, that is exactly what is happening today. That is exactly what many large Western corporations and feminist groups are doing. Instead of celebrating the brave freedom fighters who just want their personal liberty, the West celebrates the exact thing these women fight against.

Barbie, once a beacon of femininity and feminism, now dons a hijab so she won't entice men who might rape her. Marks & Spencer, one of the UK's largest department stores, and Banana Republic sells hijabs for girls. The free West, where these brave girls used to look to as beacons of light and hope, is supporting their oppressors and ultimately fighting against their progress. In Saudi Arabia, women are burning their niqabs. In Iran, women tie their hijabs on sticks and sway them silently, defiantly in the streets as they are arrested in droves. In the West, we put a Nike swoosh on hijabs.

We accept and willingly support the subjugation of our sisters to the East, even though we would never accept that for ourselves or our sisters in the West. Here, we demand that women be able to "free the nipple," but we support those in the East who demand that women "cover their head."

It is devastating to see this disconnect. Young women here are looking for a fight, and young women there desperately need fighters to stand with them. It should be a match made in sisterhood heaven. If only women were willing to link hands across borders, patriarchy would not stand a chance. Patriarchy cannot exist without the active participation of women. Men prefer to have a cut wife, but it is mothers who take their daughters to have their clitoris cut off by another woman. We hold down our screaming five-year-old daughters and allow a woman to take a razor to their genitals because a man will prefer her that way. We must stand up and say no. Mothers must stand up for their daughters. We must fight the patriarchy together instead of fighting one another. Sisters must stand up for their sisters. And neighbours must stand up for their neighbours.

For most women in Muslim-majority countries, their only options are fight, flight, or freeze. The most commonly chosen option is to freeze. *Choose* is not the right word here. Women accept rather than choose—they submit. In a world where you are a lone salmon fighting upstream in a tsunami, it is understandable that you would just submit. You accept the life mapped out for you. You marry the man chosen for you. You have his babies. Then you die with the hope that after your death you will get to leave Hell and enter Heaven.

A less commonly chosen option is to flee. There are countless stories of women who have run away from their families or their husbands and are trying to survive on their own in a new country with no family, no community, no friends, and no resources for support. It is a difficult choice. And what's even worse is that some women, like Dina Ali, don't make it. In 2017, Dina tried to escape from her family in Saudi Arabia, but in her stopover at the Manila airport, she was denied entrance to her flight to Australia. She told other passengers that she was scared for her life, that her father was coming to get her and that he would kill her. She took to Twitter and begged the world to save her, but we didn't. Dina's mouth, her hands, and her feet were duct-taped, and she was forced on a flight back to Saudi Arabia. No one has heard from her since then.

And finally, the most dangerous option: fight. Women living in oppressive societies who fight back are either silenced by their families or by the government. One of many high-profile cases is that of Loujain al-Hathloul. Loujain attended the same university in Canada that I did. After graduating, she became a fierce campaigner for women's rights in Saudi Arabia. She won many humanitarian awards for her unrelenting efforts to get women in Saudi Arabia the rights to drive, to be treated as citizens equal to men, and to abolish the guardianship laws that lock women in as eternal dependents, much like an open-air prison. According to those gender apartheid laws, a woman cannot do the most basic things without the permission of her male guardian. She must get his permission before she opens a bank account, travels, and in some cases even before she receives medical treatment! Because of her activism, Loujain was imprisoned by the state of Saudi Arabia along with a dozen other female activists.

As much as women in the Muslim world are fighting back, we will only succeed if we work together. Women in the East must work together, and women in the West—please reach back your hand and pull women in the East up the road to equality with you. Anyone who believes in freedom and equality, please support the freedom fighters in Muslim-majority countries. They need you.

ACKNOWLEDGMENTS

First and foremost, I would like to thank my husband for supporting me through the mental anguish of writing this book. Thank you for walking me in my catatonic state down to the beach to stare at the waves until I felt myself returning to my body again. Thank you for helping me get my mood back to normal by indulging my every "Do you feel like eating cupcakes? I'm in the mood for fried chicken and cupcakes." I am so glad I found you. I'm the luckiest girl in the world.

Thank you to my daughters for withstanding the random crying fits and the sudden need to write a note into my phone because a memory had just hit me. Thank you for putting up with my "Oh you think that's bad? I never had a *single birthday party* growing up" anecdotes. Thank you for being such wonderful, loving, thoughtful, caring, and absolutely most amazing girls a mommy could ever hope for.

And an extra special thank you to Sam Harris for encouraging me to still publish this book after I had lost all desire to publish it. The incessant onslaught of rejection letters and the never-ceasing hate I have been inundated with made me feel like throwing in the towel and walking away. Sam's kindness and patience and unending support is what changed my mind. You would not be reading this book if it were not for him.

Thank you to Ayaan Hirsi Ali for paving the way for all of us and for the inspiration you provide through your courage, strength, and graciousness. Without your example of bravery, I never would have had the courage to forge the path from scratch as you did. Thank you for lighting the way for me and for millions more like us. Thank you to all the other ex-Muslims out there who are brave enough to show their faces and speak up. Thank you for inspiring others to live their authentic lives, and thank you for spreading the risk! The more of us who come out, the safer we all are. You are my hero.

Thank you to Christopher Hitchens; I like to think that you would have been proud of me. I follow your example of speaking my truth regardless of which tribe it might offend. Thank you to Richard Dawkins for being one of the brave people who do not hold back on their criticism of Islam but who treat it no differently than any other religion or ideology despite the insurmountable backlash. Thank you to Dave Rubin for bringing me on your show and making me instantly forget that I was so nervous I was about to faint! Thank you to Maajid

Nawaz, Tarek Fatah, Imam Tawhidi, Asra Nomani, Raheel Raza and all the other Muslims who speak out in support of ex-Muslims and other ostracized minority groups oppressed under Sharia. I'm so honoured to know you all.

And most of all, thank you to Ben Affleck. If he hadn't had that off-the-rails tirade on Bill Maher's show, I likely never would have even bothered to take up this activism. After watching him rant incoherently at Sam Harris, I could not help but feel the same way Elaine must have felt, I am sure, in that *Seinfeld* episode where everyone was eating finger foods—including chocolate bars—with a knife and fork. She stood up and yelled: "Have you all gone mad?"

It was that feeling that propelled me into this world. How could I sit idly by as I was surrounded by people who were just being ridiculous? I needed to tell them that it was not Sam who was being gross and racist, it was Ben. He was the one who was treating people differently based on their ethnicity—the very definition of racism.

Lightning Source UK Ltd.
Milton Keynes UK
UKHW012213171022
410614UK00005B/921